SIMON SHERIDAN

Archetypology Volume 1

The Archetypal Study of Human Nature

First edition

This book was professionally typeset on Reedsy.
Find out more at reedsy.com

Contents

Preface

In a 1959 edition of the Cambridge University journal, *Blackfriars*, there is an article entitled "Some Recent Studies in Archetypology", which begins as follows:-

> There is no such word as archetypology, nor is there any one discipline which could fittingly be so named. But we might invent the word to cover all those various studies which, in very different ways, contribute to our understanding of what the analytical psychologists call archetypes - the primordial images and patterns of behaviour of a supra-personal character which the depth-psychologists find in their clinical work, and which have been expressed in manifold ways by human beings throughout the ages and throughout the world. Whatever else may be said for or against Jung's concept of the archetype, it has undoubtedly provided a meeting place for specialists in the most disparate fields of inquiry.

It seems that nobody has taken up the work presaged in the article. This is not surprising. Both Jungian psychology and holistic thinking in general have fallen out of fashion in the post-war years, despite a burst of interest in the first half of the 20th century. There are still Jungians doing work with the archetypes, but they tend to go looking for them in dreams, myths, and other dark places of the psyche, or as in the case of one of the best-known exponents of the Jungian paradigm, James Hillman, in the imagination.

I unexpectedly made my own journey into Jungian thought several years ago with the publication of my book *The Devouring Mother: The Collective Unconscious in the Age of Corona*. As the title suggests, this was an account of the covid hysteria using Jung's concept of a "mass movement" driven by a specific archetype. It was my continued attempts to work through the ramifications of that idea that led me eventually to a larger conceptual model which placed the archetypes at the centre of analysis. I had inadvertently picked up where the Blackfriars article left off about sixty-five years earlier.

I had given my framework various names during its development, none of which I was happy with, when finally the term *archetypology* popped into my head. A quick internet search led me straight to the *Blackfriars* article, which not only confirmed that the name was a good one but that the wider model was also broadly consonant with the holistic thinking from the 1950s. To use another Jungian concept, this had all the hallmarks of a synchronicity. Since the direction of the work defined in the *Blackfriars* article mirrors my own, since I had independently stumbled across the same term *archetypology*, and since it seems nobody else has used that term, I decided to adopt it as the name of the framework I have been developing and that will be presented in this book.

While archetypology has a strong grounding in Jungian thought, it differs from the Jungian approach in aiming to go beyond the psychological perspective to integrate the biological, socio-cultural, and spiritual aspects of human nature. As we will see many times in the pages ahead, the esoteric (psychological) is a complement of the exoteric (social). A holistic and integral model needs both, and that is what we aim to present. This enables us to see connections between nominally discrete domains of existence. In fairness to Freud and Jung, both men were interested in the wider ramifications of their work and wrote a number of books exploring them. In archetypology, we apply the same spirit but with a more explicitly integral approach.

It is this desire for an integrated view that connects archetypology with another intellectual movement from the 20th century, which was the search for holistic and integral models that could unify the disparate disciplines of scholarship. There is, as far as I know, only one thinker who has meaningfully progressed the domain of integral and holistic thinking in recent decades, and that is the American Ken Wilber. While Wilber's work has much in common with the ideas we will discuss, archetypology differs in that its first and foremost concern is the human individual. Wilber's earlier writings do touch on questions of individual development, but his more recent work has been concerned with what he calls the development of consciousness. Followers of Wilber should find a lot of common ground in this book but hopefully also much that is novel and unexplored in integral theory.

Archetypology may, in fact, have more in common with the concept of the archetypes that Jung pursued later in his life, especially in his collaboration with physicist Wolfgang Pauli. That was the idea that the archetypes are not just a function of human psychology but of the universe itself. We may think of this as a mathematics of the archetypes, an approach which looks for common forms and patterns. This way of thinking will be especially important in the second half of the book, where we will posit that the underlying pattern of human development is what we will call the cycle-ending-in-transcendence. This notion is consonant with the scientific discipline of biology and even some findings from physics and might have interested the older Jung for these reasons.

Although all of this implies a scholarly approach, the way of looking at human development presented in this book taps into some of the most ancient sources of wisdom, including various theological traditions, ancient myths, and history itself. We will see that the foundations of archetypology lie in two seemingly universal cultural practices: myths/stories and rites of passage. Accordingly, our main source material will not be dry scholarly papers but some of the oldest and greatest stories whose truths resonate as much today as they have over thousands of years. For this reason, this book should be of interest to a general audience rather than a specialist one.

With archetypology, we are pursuing the conjecture of the great Canadian literary critic, Northrop Frye, who speculated that the recurrent pattern found in myths and stories could provide a unifying framework for the humanities, and thereby for human nature in general. Our goal in this book is to lay out the basic shape of just such a framework and make the case for its validity.

Chapter 1: The Basic Elements of Archetypology

It was psychoanalysis which gave birth to the upsurge of interest in the archetypes in the 20th century and the followers of Carl Jung are still the most prominent exponents of archetypal analysis. In archetypology, we do not deny the validity of the psychoanalytic approach. However, our goal is to expand the scope of the archetypes beyond the psychological. For us, the archetypes are complex symbols that point not just to psychic phenomena but to biological, socio-cultural, and spiritual truths. Furthermore, the archetypes we will be concerned with are not discrete entities unrelated to each other, but interrelated parts of the sequence of human life. This was an idea that Jung briefly touched on in some of his work, but it will form the core of our model of human nature.

For those familiar with Jung's technical work, we need to be clear that the set of archetypes we are dealing with are not his components of the psyche, such as the shadow, the anima, and the animus, but what are sometimes called the character archetypes. The four primary archetypes we will use are the Child, the Orphan, the Adult, and the Elder. Each of these respectively corresponds to the phases of life that we refer to in everyday language by the names childhood, adolescence, maturity, and senescence. Since these terms are mostly used to describe the biological development that occurs over the course of our lives, they leave out the socio-cultural and higher spiritual perspectives. That is one reason why we prefer to use the archetypes themselves as symbols that represent the full range of meanings applicable to the phases of life.

The Child is about the physical, psychological, and socio-cultural aspects of childhood. The Orphan is about the physical, psychological, socio-cultural, and spiritual aspects of adolescence, and so on for the Adult and the Elder. At least for the Child and the Adult, this usage mostly matches the meanings that are associated with these words in common language. When we imagine a prototypical Child or Adult, we are capable of imagining the full range of meanings that the words evoke. The Orphan and Elder are less commonly used in ordinary discourse, but their meanings will become clear as we proceed.

Thus, in archetypology we aim to capture the broadest possible set of meanings associated with the archetypes. Normally, this would risk an overloaded set of connotations that could quickly devolve into an obscure morass. We can avoid this potential problem by introducing just a few core concepts that give our framework both clarity and flexibility. One of the most important planks of that structure, one that we will use time and again throughout the book, is the distinction between the exoteric and the esoteric.

Exoteric means outward-facing, while esoteric means inward-facing. While the inner and outer aspects of our lives can be mirrors of each other, it's also true that they can operate separately. Usually from late childhood onwards, we learn to hide some of our inner feelings and thoughts from the outside world. Meanwhile, those around us, who must always judge from our outward expression, can misinterpret the signals we send and draw the wrong conclusions about our inner states. In fact, this happens all the time and is one of the main drivers of both the drama and the comedy of life.

In this book, we will use the word *esoteric* to denote all the inner aspects of human existence, including emotions, feelings, desires, dreams, thoughts, the will, and the intellect. We also include here any unconscious aspects of the psyche as well as theological concepts such as soul and spirit.

By contrast, the *exoteric* refers to all the outer aspects of human existence, such as our physiological appearance determined by our biological inheritance, our social aspect as marked by clothing and styling, our mannerisms, the way we walk, the way we talk, and anything else that a third-party observer can see, and who a third-party observer knows better than we do, since we do not see ourselves *objectively*.

Let's mark this distinction onto an x-axis as follows:-

Esoteric ⟵――――――――――――――――――――――――――⟶ Exoteric

We will now plot the second main structural plank of our analytical framework onto the y-axis.

The concepts that we are about to invoke have a very long tradition in philosophy and theology. They are sometimes referred to as the great chain of being or the levels of being. Traditionally, there are four elements defined. We will leave out the physical level of being, as it has little bearing on our framework. The three remaining levels we will refer to as the biological, the socio-cultural and the higher esoteric. We can plot these against the esoteric-exoteric distinction on a y-axis as follows:-

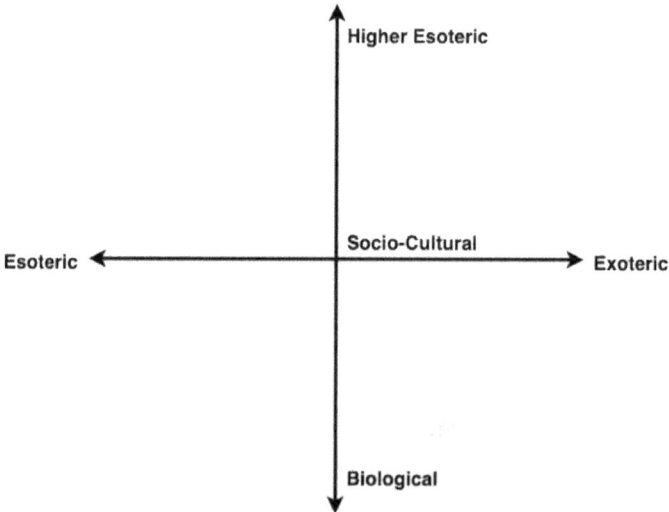

Higher Esoteric

Esoteric ⟵――――――――――――――⟶ Exoteric
Socio-Cultural

Biological

We can then read off the diagram to better grasp the differences between the levels of being as they relate to their esoteric and exoteric aspects.

The exoteric aspect of the biological level of being refers to our inheritance as members of the species *homo sapiens*, with the specific genetic endowment received from our parents being the most decisive for shaping our external appearance in terms of skin, eye, and hair colour; height; weight; body type; and so on.

The esoteric side of the biological can be thought of as the bottom rung of Maslow's famous hierarchy of needs. These are the feelings and emotions that derive from the biological necessities of life. We feel hungry, thirsty, tired, energetic, cold, hot, etc.

Those familiar with Maslow's hierarchy will see that his higher needs pertain directly to the higher levels of being we have identified, e.g., a sense of belonging maps to the socio-cultural level of being. However, rather than framing these in terms of *needs*, we will use a different way of thinking about them. We will call them our *identities*. Thus, we have biological, socio-cultural, and higher esoteric identities. The combination of these creates our *character*.

The distinction between esoteric and exoteric refers to the inner and outer aspects of our character, and this can be divided between the biological, the socio-cultural, and the higher esoteric identities. Life can be thought of as the continual creation and recreation of our character through the tension that flows back and forth between the esoteric and the exoteric. This tension oscillates around an equilibrium at each of the levels of being. Hunger and thirst are the esoteric signals that our body needs food and water. Cold and tiredness are signals that we need heat and rest, and so on. These can all be said to resonate at the biological level of being.

At the next level up, we have the socio-cultural level of being. The exoteric dimension here refers to properties such as our style of clothing, our class and economic position, our career, our political and religious affiliation, and so on. Each of these exoteric components has an esoteric aspect. A wedding ring is an exoteric symbol of marriage, but to know whether the relationship is characterised by esoteric feelings of love and affection or frustration and resentment requires a level of intimacy that is usually hidden from public sight. The same is true for the other aspects of our socio-cultural identity.

Are we stimulated or bored at work? Do we respect and trust our political institutions or believe them to be corrupt and decadent? Does our religion provide us with feelings of awe and wonder or only hollow words and empty ceremonies?

The esoteric and exoteric need to find an equilibrium. When they do not, it is possible that the exoteric structure breaks down. With modern divorce laws, a loveless marriage, which is an esoteric signal that something is wrong, can quickly turn into divorce; the disintegration of the exoteric union. The same is true of a boring job, a corrupt political system, and a meaningless religious practice, all of which have an exoteric form that can break apart if the esoteric goes missing. Conversely, it can occur that the exoteric structure does not break down but a variety of esoteric pathologies ensue instead, including everything from basic negative emotions such as irritability and anger, through to dissociation and other states that we now call *mental illness*.

Our third level of being is the higher esoteric and this seems to break our esoteric-exoteric dichotomy since it is, by definition, esoteric in nature. Most theologies hold that the higher esoteric is the connection with the divine and therefore has no material form. However, the higher esoteric must also connect with the material plane of this world too. This issue is at the core of the Christian theology, which, in our terminology, holds that the higher esoteric was made exoteric in the person of Jesus.

The category of the higher esoteric touches on all the ancient questions of theology, philosophy, and psychology. We are going to approach these in an indirect fashion from within the archetypology framework itself later in the book. For now, let's simply note that by the higher esoteric we refer to theological concepts such as spirit and soul, philosophical concepts such as virtue, happiness, justice, and beauty, and psychological concepts such as ego, consciousness, and the collective unconscious. What each of these has in common is that they have no material existence and aren't obviously related to either the biological or socio-cultural levels of being (again, setting aside a number of long-standing philosophical and theological debates on the subject).

There is one aspect of the higher esoteric that is worth mentioning at this point, and that is a pattern which shows up numerous times in religious history as a dramatic spiritual upheaval in an individual. Consider St. Paul's *road to Damascus* moment, St. Francis of Assisi and Buddha's sudden break with civilisation, Mohammed's visit by the archangel Gabriel, Jesus' confrontation with the devil, and so on. All of these, and other mystical experiences, can be described as a direct encounter with the higher esoteric. However, they also trigger a transformation in the life of the person in question. We can characterise that transformation using the concept discussed by Jesus in the Bible as being *born again*. What Jesus means is that we need to be born again in spirit, which we can translate into our terminology as being born again at the higher esoteric level of being.

However, what archetypology shows is that the born again paradigm also holds at the biological and socio-cultural levels of being. Even if we limit ourselves just to the biological level of being, nobody would deny that childhood, adolescence, maturity, and senescence are all qualitatively different phases. It follows that there must be a metamorphosis, or born again event, that separates them. But this metamorphosis occurs at all three levels of being, and the qualitative change that it initiates is a change of archetype. It may sound overly dramatic, but the born again pattern holds when applied to the archetypes. We die as a Child and are reborn as an Orphan. We die as an Orphan and are reborn as Adult etc.

Each of these rebirths produces a qualitative transformation in our character over and above the normal oscillation between the esoteric and exoteric poles of the biological, socio-cultural, and higher esoteric levels of being. What the archetypes signify is a shift in focus that gives each phase of life its unique quality. The transition from one archetype to the next breaks us out of equilibrium and thrusts us into a completely new paradigm. We are *born again* each time.

With these very brief introductory remarks, we have defined the core concepts of archetypology that we will use repeatedly in this book. Let's summarise them here for maximum clarity:-

- Archetype: a discrete phase of life consisting of qualitatively distinct

properties of character formation. The four primary archetypes are Child, Orphan, Adult, and Elder
- Character: the dynamic interaction between the three primary identities of biological, socio-cultural, and higher esoteric
- Identity: a process that oscillates between the exoteric and esoteric poles, driven by the inner needs and desires of the individual and the collective influence of environment, society, and any higher powers that one believes in

What we are aiming for is a high-level map of human development. Like any good map, it should chart out the main features of the terrain while also allowing the map holder to zoom in where necessary. In this chapter we have taken just an overview of the main features of our map. We will spend the rest of the book exploring it in more detail as we describe the archetypal study of human nature.

Chapter 2: The Development of Character

Let's begin by recapping the main concepts we introduced in the last chapter. We said that the archetypes are qualitatively distinct phases of life. We then defined two sets of criteria that allow us to understand that quality. Firstly, there are the three domains of identity—the biological, socio-cultural, and higher esoteric. Secondly, there is the exoteric-esoteric distinction, which can be applied to the domains of identity to give six broad categories of analysis.

This framework of analysis can be applied to issues that are not intrinsically related to the archetypes. Consider the question of hunger. Nobody would deny that hunger is an esoteric emotion that (usually) relates to the exoteric biological fact of needing nutrition. That is how we would define it at the biological level as it pertains to the individual. However, if hunger affects an entire society (famine), then we would say it belongs to the socio-cultural domain. This may result in a social crisis that can play out in any number of unpleasant ways. Similarly, we also know that a prolonged and severe famine can lead to the questioning of the higher esoteric beliefs of a culture, or at least requires some explanation in terms of those beliefs, e.g., God is punishing us. Each of these is a qualitatively different manifestation of what is, in some sense, the same phenomenon. In this chapter, we will be performing this kind of analysis on the archetypes themselves to get a better understanding of their qualitative differences.

The other main analytical tool we will be applying relates to the third concept we introduced previously: the notion of being *born again*. The word we will use to capture that concept is *metamorphosis*. In order to transition between the qualitatively different phases of life known as archetypes, there must be a metamorphosis. Since we have defined four archetypes, it follows that there are at least four metamorphoses that we go through in the course of life. These metamorphoses can also be analysed using both the domains of identity and the esoteric-exoteric distinction. For example, when we come of age, we are expected to take a role in society. The beginning of that process comes with a variety of new esoteric experiences, including nervousness, uncertainty, and anxiety, but also excitement. These are usually tied to a variety of exoteric occurrences called rites of passage, a concept that we will investigate in detail in the second half of the book. All these developments take place in the socio-cultural domain. But the coming-of-age metamorphosis also takes place at the biological and higher esoteric domains too. We will investigate both of these later in the chapter.

The overall pattern we see is that each archetypal phase begins with a metamorphosis and then settles down into a long period of stability. The metamorphosis is the time of highest risk because what is at stake is the reconfiguration of our character, which takes place across the levels of being and between the exoteric and esoteric aspects of existence. We are not used to thinking about them in this way, but the metamorphoses really are about being *born again*. If that's true, then we might say that the archetypes represent mini-lives. Each mini-life has its own mission, its own challenges, and its own opportunities. In this chapter and the next, we will analyse the primary qualities of these mini-lives that we call the archetypes. Let's begin.

The Child Archetype

Undoubtedly, it was the Oedipus Complex which raised the issue of child psychology to the prominent position it was to enjoy throughout the 20th century. At the same time that Freud and Jung were making their breakthroughs in psychoanalysis, G. Stanley Hall was laying the foundations for modern developmental psychology. There followed an avalanche of scholarship on the question of childhood development, including the work of Piaget, Vygotsky, B.F. Skinner, and numerous others.

Curiously, this focus on childhood had already appeared in other social trends. These days, we take the literary genre of children's books for granted. But this is also a relatively recent development, beginning in earnest in the 19th century. Prior to that, to the extent that anything that could be called children's literature existed, its purpose was to inculcate moral lessons in the young. Fictional representations of childhood, which aimed to depict the spirit of that phase of life and which we see in modern writers like Roald Dahl and Dr. Seuss or characters such as Harry Potter and Tom Sawyer, simply didn't exist.

Alongside these developments emerged the idea that life required the nurturance of the *inner child* and that the danger of adulthood was precisely that we lost the sense of wonder, inquisitiveness, and imagination that is associated with childhood. This idea is implied in the work of the English poet Wordsworth, the German composer Wagner, the Russian novelist Dostoevsky, and the American psychologist Eric Berne, to name a few.

As a result of all this, it's fair to say that our era has an appreciation and care for the Child archetype that might be unique in history. It's not uncommon to find cultures throughout history where children were considered to be not yet fully human. It seems plausible that such attitudes were related to the fact that child mortality has traditionally been very high, which meant that overly sentimental attachments to children would be quite likely to cause distress and despair given the relatively high chance of death. Our modern focus on childhood may be closely related to the advances that have made child mortality decline radically.

From an archetypology point of view, the Child archetype provides an ideal starting point to demonstrate our assertion that the pattern of every archetypal phase is a dramatic metamorphosis followed by a long period of stability. If we think about the biological level of being, the period from conception to birth is the most dramatic biological metamorphosis of our lives. Only slightly less radical is the period of growth that begins after birth and continues for the first several years. Eventually, the frantic pace of growth ends, and childhood settles down into the kind of stability that fills the pages of children's literature and film, a period of adventure and play that seems like it will go on forever.

We have said that the metamorphosis is the period of highest risk, and the aforementioned question of child mortality justifies this claim. Even with modern medical advances, the period immediately after birth has the highest risk of death. This falls precipitously so that a Child that has reached their second birthday is statistically almost certain to live a full life. Alongside the issue of mortality, modern developmental theory posits a number of critical periods for physical and neurological development. The failure to meet these timelines can often result in lifelong problems. Again, it is mostly in the first few years that we see such issues emerge, and this justifies our statement that once the metamorphosis period is over, we see a long period of stability. That is certainly true at the biological level for the Child archetype.

At the other two levels of being, the resonance of the Child archetype is not entirely missing but is very much less important than the biological. Certainly for the first year or two of life, there is almost nothing that we would categorise as socio-cultural or higher esoteric development. Moreover, the development that occurs after that is almost entirely limited to the family sphere. Seemingly every society acknowledges this fact by leaving the care of the Child to its parents during this time. Even in communitarian ancient Sparta, the Child was only removed from the household and placed in public education at six years of age. Societies give no legal, economic, or political status to children except as wards of their parents, and most children are not interested in pursuing an identity of their own anyway and will instinctively return to the safety of the family if left alone.

What we mean when we say that the Child does not resonate at the socio-cultural and higher esoteric is that the individual does not experience these domains. However, it is true to say that there is a metamorphosis of sorts, although it is one that is for the benefit of family and society. The anthropological literature shows that almost every society has a set of rites and ceremonies that are conducted for the Child. Some variation of baptism is a very common practice across different cultures, for example. These socio-cultural practices are always tied in with the belief structure of the higher esoteric, and so we can say that they are a metamorphosis that resonates at both the socio-cultural and higher esoteric domains. However, that metamorphosis is not understood by the Child itself. Rather, these practices are intended to mark to the parents and to other members of society that a new member has arrived.

In terms of personal development, it is true that the Child evolves a personality and other qualities such as intelligence, especially during the second half of childhood, and we would say that these resonate in the higher esoteric domain. Note, however, that these come later in the archetypal phase, and they are based around repetition and mimicry rather than the expression of individuality. We might, therefore, categorise them as belonging more to the biological level of being than the higher esoteric since they seem to be based in instinct. Of the psychic state of the Child, Jung wrote, "It is as though it were not yet completely born, but were still enclosed in the psychic atmosphere of its parents." Jung's use of the metaphor of birth here is telling. Birth is a metamorphosis at the biological level of being. What Jung is saying is that the Child has no corresponding metamorphosis at the psychic level.

Thus, if we think about these matters in terms of our metamorphosis-stability pattern, we would say that the Child has a metamorphosis at the biological level primarily, while any correspondence at the socio-cultural and higher esoteric levels is only preparatory in nature. The real emergence of character in these latter domains does not occur until the onset of the Orphan archetype at puberty. Jung was certainly correct in saying that the Child's psyche is dominated by that of its parents, but the same is true of its socio-cultural identity. As we have already pointed out, it seems to be a universal of human affairs that children are given no social status independent of their parents. This leads to the generalisation that all of the Child's development is tied to the family, including the biological sphere.

This is true in two ways. Firstly, the Child's biological development is predicated on the provision of nourishment and care that the parents are expected to provide. The family unit exists, in very large part, for the raising of children. Therefore, the family is responsible for creating the environment that allows the Child's biological development. The second way that biological identity is tied to the family is because it is the institution that is predicated on genetic relationships of inheritance and is therefore fundamentally biological in nature. The family has other functions, including economic, legal, and even religious, but all of these serve to propagate the biological relationships.

In short, practically all development of the Child, whether biological, socio-cultural, or higher esoteric, takes place within the family. So dominant is the family's influence over the Child that it can often lead to feelings of resentment, especially in the second half of childhood, where the Child begins to dream of an identity of its own. This resentment is present in Freud's famous *Oedipus Complex* but is also a core feature of children's stories. The desire to escape the domination of the parents is implied in many European fairy tales where the Child comes to ruin by going off alone. Meanwhile, the oppressive and domineering parent figure is a mainstay of both fairy tales and modern children's literature. Just think of any Roald Dahl children's story, and chances are that it features an ugly and deformed parent, the physical representation being a symbol of the Child's resentment.

But, of course, the Child cannot become independent in any meaningful way. The family exists to allow the Child to develop, and where it does not exist or is malfunctioning in some way, we rightfully view this as an existential threat and most societies will have some mechanism to address the problem, usually by finding a substitute family. The structure and nature of the family may vary a lot between cultures, but whatever form the family takes, care of the Child is one of its main functions.

For these reasons, and others that will become clearer later, we will combine the biological and familial domains into a single strand of identity called, unsurprisingly, the *biological-familial*. This identity then encompasses almost the full spectrum of character development that occurs during the Child archetypal phase. It is true that, especially in the second half of childhood, the Child has friends and usually receives some form of education and initiation into society. But all of this is rudimentary and limited in scope. The main development of the Child takes place in the family, in its relations with its parents and siblings, and primarily through the biological growth that occurs mostly in the instinctual realm.

Although the biological-familial domain represents the entirety of the Child's character development, it is also true that our identity in this domain evolves over the course of our lives. Therefore, we can map the biological-familial in diagram form as follows, showing the metamorphosis which initiates each archetypal phase for this domain:-

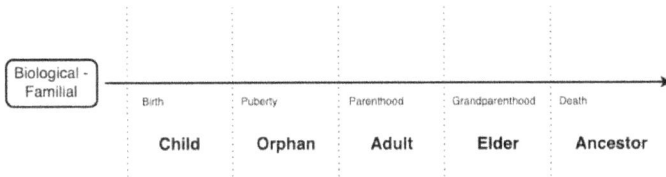

Later in the chapter, we will add additional strands to our diagram as we show that our identity expands beyond the biological-familial in the archetypal phases that follow the Child. We will also analyse how our biological-familial identity modifies for each subsequent archetype.

Summing up, we say that the metamorphosis that initiates the Child archetype resonates primarily at the biological-familial level of being. To the extent that we can find socio-cultural metamorphoses in baptism or other similar rituals, these are not important to the Child who is unable to understand them, but they are important to the broader society and especially the family by symbolising the arrival of a new member. The Child is thrown into the world completely dependent on the family. The family is the cocoon in which its development can proceed safely and stably. In the normal course of events, this cocoon is broken at the time of puberty, with an eruption of character development across all domains. The individual must break forth from the family unit and forge their own identity in the broader society. That is the metamorphosis which signals the arrival of the next archetype in the series: the Orphan.

The Orphan Archetype

Just as interest in the Child archetype is a relatively recent phenomenon in Western culture, the closely related Orphan archetype is also a new arrival on the scene, at least as far as its appearance in literature and storytelling is concerned. The 19th century was the time when the children's book became popular, but it also marked the beginning of the *bildungsroman*, or coming-of-age story. Technically speaking, we can find Orphan heroes in stories going back to antiquity, but the coming-of-age story was somewhat different in focusing on the trials and tribulations of the teenage years in their own terms. It's not a coincidence that it was around the same time that Shakespeare enjoyed a surge in popularity, especially his Orphan heroes Romeo, Juliet, Hamlet, and Ophelia. We can think of this age as a precursor to the arrival of the *teenager* in the 20th century.

Whether or not the Orphan is recognised by the wider culture, its place in the sequence of archetypes is established not just by literary but, perhaps more importantly, by anthropological facts. Across cultures, the onset of puberty is marked as the beginning of a new phase of life, and the most obvious reason is because it results in sexual maturity, which brings all kinds of complications and dangers. From our archetypal point of view, however, the general theme of the Orphan phase of life can be found in the name of the archetype itself. The names of the other archetypes are straightforward and uncontroversial. Child, Adult, and Ancestor are everyday words. Elder is less well-known, but its meaning is self-explanatory. Orphan is the only one of our archetypal names that is metaphorical.

In everyday language, the word *orphan* denotes a person whose parents have died. Metaphorically, something very similar happens during the Orphan phase of life. The symbolism of the death of the parent is very common in the literature and rites that revolve around the Orphan and seems to be a universal of human culture. For example, in medieval European myths, the young knight who is about to go on a great quest usually has one or both parents dead. Hamlet's father is dead in Shakespeare's great play, while Hamlet himself will accidentally kill Ophelia's father, thereby making her an orphan too. Hansel and Gretel's mother has died. So has Cinderella's. Harry Potter's parents are dead. So are Luke Skywalker's and Batman's. The symbolic meaning of the death of the parent in these stories is that the Child is now on their own. They have no option but to venture forth into the world and make their own way. That is the Orphan's mission.

Alongside the countless literary examples, anthropology also provides ample evidence for the separation from the parents that occurs at the beginning of the Orphan phase of life. The Australian Aboriginal initiation given to boys is particularly instructive in this respect. Initiation begins with the boy being quite literally removed from the arms of his mother and taken away by the men of the tribe. The mother ceremoniously wails and cries, signalling the fact that she is losing her child and their relationship will be forever changed. On the other side of initiation, the family relationship still exists, but the boy is now under the tutelage of an older man whose job is to ensure his journey to adulthood is successful. The parents are no longer the main influence; the boy must establish himself in the wider society.

These facts lend extra weight to our decision in the last section to combine the biological with the familial identities. The symbolic death of the Parent captures the fact that their domination is over and that the Orphan must break free from the restrictions of the biological-familial realm. This process is assisted by the wider society, which, until this time, has been content to leave the Child with its Parents, but now offers a variety of new roles and identities to the Orphan. Each of these must be pursued outside the family.

But we shouldn't be fooled into thinking that the Orphan phase of life is something that is only imposed on the Child from without. On the contrary, with the onset of puberty, our character suddenly springs into being at seemingly all identities simultaneously, and the desire to create it comes from within. Alongside the biological metamorphosis, there is the sudden arrival of what psychoanalysts call the ego, representing a definitive change at the higher esoteric level of being. This is how Jung describes the psychological changes that occur at the beginning of the Orphan period:-

> *Psychic birth, and with it the conscious distinction of the ego from the parents, takes place in the normal course of things at the age of puberty with the eruption of sexual life. The physiological change is attended by a psychic revolution. For the various bodily manifestations give such an emphasis to the ego that it often asserts itself without stint or measure.*

This is sometimes called 'the unbearable age'.

Thus, unlike the Child metamorphosis, which is experienced only at the biological level of being, the Orphan metamorphosis consists of the biological transformation of puberty and the higher esoteric arrival of the ego. It is a psychic birth, a birth of sexuality, and, as we will see, a socio-cultural birth. The Orphan phase of life represents the beginning of the resonance of our character across all available dimensions of identity. But, of course, we do not immediately become a fully-formed Adult. The Orphan is the intermediate phase between the Child and the Adult as we begin to feel our way towards what will eventually become our mature character. It is a time of initiation, education, and training.

Since the Orphan encompasses the full spectrum of identities, it allows us to outline each of those domains in more detail. Let's take them one by one and see how they develop during the Orphan phase of life.

Sexual Identity

The biological metamorphosis of puberty represents, among other things, the onset of sexual maturity. Most societies have tight restrictions around the expression of sexuality at this time in order to channel it into the formation of a new family unit via marriage. In these cases, we could subsume sexual identity within our already established category of biological-familial. However, some societies allow for the development of a sexual identity outside of the confines of the family. This is especially true in the modern West. Thus, it makes sense to add sexual identity to our diagram, which we do as follows:-

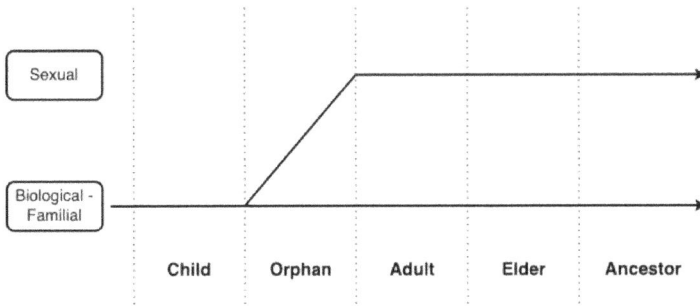

The anthropological literature shows a number of different practices around sexuality, many of which are deeply distasteful, if not downright disgusting, to our modern sensibility. Because of the sensitive nature of the subject, there is no need to dwell on them here except to say that the range of sexual identities that the Orphan may take is much more varied than the default social scripts of the modern West, even considering the fairly radical loosening of sexual norms in the post-war years.

Despite all of the differences in sexual identity that can be seen across cultures, it should not be a surprise from our point of view to find that the metamorphosis that signifies the real beginning of sexual identity is the loss of virginity. Here we must touch on a subject that modern feminism has raised, which is that the most common pattern across cultures and throughout history has been that women are expected to remain virgins until marriage while men often have no such restriction. This is not a universal of human culture, but it is the predominant pattern. What this means is that women have been required to only express their sexual identity within the confines of the family. In terms of our above diagram, we would not draw a separate line of identity for women since they are expected to have no independent sexual identity.

What these traditional differences between the sexes amount to is not a difference of form but of timing. The loss of virginity is still the meta-morphosis that ushers in sexual identity. The question is whether it occurs during the Orphan phase of life or the Adult phase (i.e., before or after marriage). However, this point quickly becomes moot when we realise that the asymmetry between the sexes on the question of virginity maps to a similar asymmetry in relation to marriage. This leads us naturally into the next domain of identity: the biological-familial.

Biological-Familial

The points just made about how female sexual identity has traditionally been expressed only within the confines of marriage need to be understood against a closely related social practice whereby women have been married shortly after puberty. Within our model, marriage is the initiation into the biological-familial domain that signifies the beginning of the Adult phase of life. The fact that the average age of marriage for women has traditionally been much younger than for men signifies that the Orphan phase of life has been shorter for women.

Here we find a second important reason why we have differentiated between the biological-familial domain and the socio-cultural. The socio-cultural consists of all the institutions of society outside of the family, including the economic, political, military, and religious. As modern feminists have correctly pointed out, women have traditionally been denied access to some of those institutions, especially the political and military ones. Women's place has been the family. What's more, we can see that the expression of a woman's sexual and economic identity also takes place within the household to the extent that a woman's sexual identity has been synonymous with marriage. This follows from the fact that the household has been a major source of economic production. In fact, the word *economy* comes from the Greek *oikonomia*, which means "household management". Women may have traditionally been excluded from the forms of economic production that took place outside of the home, but they were central to the production inside it.

All of this may seem to suggest that the Orphan period of life has been very short for women. If the Orphan phase begins with puberty and women are married shortly thereafter, signalling the beginning of the Adult archetype, then not much time exists in between. That is certainly true. However, that does not mean that the Orphan metamorphosis does not occur for women.

On the contrary, we might state that it is more pronounced for women than for men.

Remember that the main theme of the Orphan archetype is the separation from the parents. A woman leaves the house of her parents to move into her husband's house. She relinquishes the surname of her family and takes that of her husband's. Often, the woman must leave the village or town where she grew up and travel to a location she is unfamiliar with, leaving behind her childhood friends and wider family. In times without modern communication technology, this could mean a complete break with the family for the rest of her life. We can see that the break with the parents and the family is far more extreme in such a scenario and that, if anything, the Orphan period is more difficult for women in such circumstances.

It is not a surprise, therefore, to find that the female Orphan archetype is captured in many fairy tales and myths via the story of the girl who is either sent away from her family or becomes a kind of outcast in her own home due to the arrival of a stepmother. In either case, the young woman finds that she must establish herself in a strange and hostile family environment. That has been the dominant pattern for women throughout history. The Orphan initiation for them has been in the biological-familial domain.

By contrast, men have had to find their identity outside the family in what we have called the socio-cultural domain. Let's now explore that in more detail.

Socio-Cultural Identity

We have already noted that the family and the household have a number of functions that we would call economic, political, legal, and sometimes even religious. What we define as the socio-cultural domain are the institutions and cultural practices that exist outside of the family. Specifically, we include economic, political, and military subcategories within this broader classification. These three almost always fit together in practice. A citizen of a society has the obligation to contribute economically (e.g., via taxation), militarily, and politically to the institutions of that society. It is at the onset of the Adult period of life when full membership and the full set of rights and responsibilities are received. As with other aspects of identity, the Orphan phase represents the beginning of the process of working towards the mature identity.

When we think about how the metamorphosis-stability pattern manifests in relation to the socio-cultural domain, we must understand that there is a dual operation at work in that the metamorphosis exists to induct the individual into the social institution. It is as much about signalling membership to others as it is about setting the expectations of the initiate. Therefore, socio-cultural metamorphoses are usually carried out in formal rites and ceremonies. We can give these the general label of *initiation,* since the word has the connotation of admitting a beginner to an institution with the intent of training them. The meaning of this is clearest in relation to the military since nobody expects a new recruit to have the fighting skills required for full membership. They must be initiated and then trained. The same is true in the economic sphere, where occupations require a set of skills that must be learned. Let's look at a few cross-cultural and historical examples of Orphan initiation.

In medieval Europe, a young man (it was always a man) would participate in a formal ceremony that required him to pledge economic, political, and military allegiance to his local lord. This was the formal beginning of his identity in those domains, and it conferred on him certain rights and responsibilities. Meanwhile, hunter-gatherer societies often had an extended initiation ritual that could last many months whereby the young man would be given instruction into the culture of the tribe, which had been mostly hidden from him when he was young. We see similar extended initiation rites in ancient Crete and other cultures around the world.

A kind of initiation that we would recognise more readily is the formal educational institutions of ancient Greece, whose explicit purpose was to prepare the student for entry into the Adult world. The two most famous examples were the Spartan *agoge* and the Athenian *ephebia.* In both cases, the instruction was specifically about civic political participation and military training, two concepts that went hand in hand at that time. This included significant physical tests of endurance and skill, real-world practical tasks, and formal ceremonies that signified induction and graduation. Our modern education system is in many ways different from the ancient Greeks, but the formal nature of the institutions is shared. This includes a special form of dress, a specific location for instruction, and a specific title. We call them *students*. The Athenians called them *ephebes*, which meant a young man undergoing military training in preparation for citizenship and, therefore, adulthood.

At this point, it is worth remarking on several ways in which the modern West's approach to the Orphan phase of life differs from these historical examples. The first is that we have swapped formal rites of passage for bureaucratic criteria. In ancient Greece, one had to go through the *ephebia* to become a citizen. Successful graduation conferred on you the rights and responsibilities involved. In the modern West, you are a citizen by default and attain full rights at certain ages specified in law. For example, you may be able to vote at eighteen years of age. Similarly, the payment of tax (your economic contribution) is handled entirely through bureaucratic and administrative systems. All of this happens automatically and doesn't require a formal initiation process.

Meanwhile, our modern education system does not confer a particular identity upon graduation. This is true of high school and has become increasingly true of university. Even specialised degrees do not automatically confer a status; they simply open the pathway to the employment opportunities. This is different from the ancient Greek and even the tribal initiations we have mentioned above. Graduation from those bestowed a quite specific change of status on the individual. The closest parallel we have from the modern world is perhaps the trade apprenticeship. Graduation from an electrical apprenticeship makes one an electrician, for example.

When viewed in this way, the relative absence of formal rites and ceremonies in the modern West as well as the mostly voluntary nature of participation can be seen as the expression of a deeper cultural belief that the individual should only do that which they are (esoterically) interested in. This belief has become even more entrenched in the post-war years and constitutes a good deal of what most people understand by the word "freedom". Both military and political involvement are as good as optional in most western nations, meaning that participation is based on personal (esoteric) motivation. Similarly, there is a great deal of freedom over what kind of economic identity one decides to pursue, and this is also predicated on the idea that the individual should do what interests them.

Thus, we can say that the modern West prioritises the esoteric over the exoteric. Nevertheless, this does not mean that the formation of identity during the Orphan period of life does not proceed. Our first job can be seen as our initiation into the economic sphere. Our first vote, or our first interest in politics, can be seen as our initiation into the political realm. If we choose to participate in the military, we receive initiation there. The same goes for less obvious but also important institutions of civil society, such as sports clubs or other voluntary associations that we choose to join. These all constitute initiation.

The important point to understand, however, is that all these are about initiation into society as distinct from the family. The Orphan must learn to receive instruction from those who are not their parents. They must learn to get along with others, especially their fellow Orphans, and they must ideally learn to care for and cherish the institutions into which they have been inducted. All of these new social expectations bring with them feelings of anxiety, excitement, and the desire to fit in. That is what the development of socio-cultural identity means for the Orphan. It is about finding one's place in wider society.

Higher Esoteric Identity

We now need to tackle a difficulty that we touched on in chapter one. We have just talked about the set of socio-cultural institutions that the Orphan must be initiated in, and we have restricted this set of institutions to the political, military, and economic realms. There is, of course, a very important set of institutions that are also, technically speaking, social in nature, and those are the religious ones. These institutions tend to follow the initiation-education pattern we have just mentioned. In fact, religious institutions often have the most elaborate and intricate forms of initiation. This raises the question of why we did not include them in the socio-cultural domain.

To a large extent, we are going to be answering that question gradually as we proceed throughout the book, and therefore we will attempt only an introductory explanation here. The foremost reason to separate the religious institutions of society is because those institutions correspond to what we have called the higher esoteric domain. This is the sphere of life that is concerned with the big questions of philosophy, theology, and science. But it also very much corresponds to modern psychology. The big questions of philosophy and the divine revelations of theology and science begin as a personal transformation before becoming part of the wider culture. A big part of the transformation that ushers in these paradigm shifts occurs in the psychological realm. That is why we need to list psychology alongside philosophy, theology, and science in what we are calling the higher esoteric domain. We will shortly provide a specific example of how this works, one that relates directly to the Orphan archetype.

Although the higher esoteric is always esoteric by default, it is nevertheless the case that there exist social institutions and roles in any society whose purpose is to guard and propagate the higher esoteric beliefs of the culture in just the same way that the political, economic, and military institutions do for their respective domains. These represent the exoteric aspect of the higher esoteric domain. Now, this raises the question of what we should call these institutions, and we are going to take the deliberately provocative move of calling them religious. That is, we are going to give the name of *religion* to the set of institutions that claim to speak on behalf of the higher esoteric beliefs of the culture in question.

The reason why we need to use this somewhat clumsy nomenclature is because we are trying to abstract away from any specific culture and society. We are trying to use words that are not tied down into a specific view of the higher esoteric or a specific historical institution that claims to speak on behalf of it. This is difficult because, unless we make up entirely new words, any words we use will have an existing connotation. To be clear, let's repeat the definitions again. By *religion,* we refer to the exoteric institutions that claim to speak on behalf of the higher esoteric. By *higher esoteric,* we refer to the belief structure itself, which revolves around ideas that, in the modern world, are encompassed by the disciplines of theology, philosophy, psychology, and science.

Thus, we can look at a culture such as ancient Greece and identify its higher esoteric beliefs as well as the institutions that propagated them. The latter includes religious schools and, later, the philosophers. We might include literature and art as well, since in their highest forms they also deal with the big questions of life. We can do the same for medieval Europe, where the Catholic Church was the dominant exoteric institution representing the higher esoteric belief structure of the Christian theology. And we can do the same for our time, where we say that the technocracy (universities, schools, bureaucracies) is the exoteric institutional form that promulgates the higher esoteric belief structure of scientific materialism.

In relation to the Orphan archetype, we can now see that the Orphan receives a religious initiation into an exoteric institution that provides an introduction to the higher esoteric belief structures of the culture. That can include a hunter-gatherer tribal initiation, it can include an ancient Athenian education in the *ephebia,* or it can include a modern education in high school and university. That seems straightforward, but we should be aware that a lot of what is learned in such settings comes more from what is implied by the education than what is communicated explicitly. Another reason to call belief structures *esoteric* is because they are mostly hidden.

At the beginning of this section, we quoted Jung, who stated that there is a psychic birth of the ego that co-occurs with puberty. This is the individual metamorphosis at the higher esoteric that brings in the Orphan phase of life. However, this way of framing the event already implies a belief structure. In the West, we know that because we have a direct point of comparison in the older belief structure that used to dominate our culture. The Christian theology recognises the exact same event that occurs at the beginning of the Orphan phase. What Jung refers to as the psychic birth of the ego is called the infusion of the Holy Spirit in the Christian belief system. Both of these refer to nominally the same metamorphosis in the individual, but they imply very different ways of understanding that event.

Now, we are not going to ask which of these is more "correct" or "accurate"; we simply note that each explanation makes sense within a belief structure that we call the higher esoteric, and we note that there is an exoteric institution which upholds that belief structure. Nobody would deny that the Catholic Church is a long-standing exoteric institution. What we have to understand is that psychoanalysis is also part of an exoteric structure that we call the technocracy. It is less formal, less centralised, and less overt than the Catholic Church, but it exists nonetheless. As members of modern Western culture, we are initiated into that belief structure in high school and university.

We are now ready to understand in more detail what it means for the Orphan to receive religious initiation. Every culture recognises the personal psychological event that takes place at the beginning of the Orphan phase of life. That event belongs to the higher esoteric domain. But alongside that metamorphosis comes the induction into the religious institutions of society. It is partly the purpose of that induction to make sense of the personal psychological event. What is being taught, therefore, is just a specific explanation but an entire worldview.

Let's again use the Catholic Church as an example. The Catholic rite of passage that occurs at the beginning of the Orphan phase is called Confirmation. The explicit purpose of this rite is to instil the Holy Spirit into the initiate. From our modern way of looking at it, this rite is superfluous. We say that the psychic birth of the ego occurs anyway. It doesn't require a rite or ceremony. Even if that is true, however, we can see that the purpose of Confirmation is to induct the initiate into the religion and thereby into the belief structure of the culture. It communicates to the initiate the meaning of the psychological event in the context of a belief structure at the higher esoteric level of being.

When we view it from this more neutral point of view, we can see that the explanation that psychoanalysis gives is also there to make sense of the psychic event. It also communicates a belief structure. The Orphan initiate is going through a psychic metamorphosis. The Catholic priest says that what is happening is the arrival of the Holy Spirit. The psychoanalyst says that what is happening is the psychic birth of the ego. Each of these explanations is tied to a framework of understanding that exists in the higher esoteric and to an exoteric institutional structure that promulgates them. The priest is the representative of the Catholic Church. The psychoanalyst is the representative of the technocracy. To the extent that the Orphan sees the psychoanalyst as the legitimate authority, they will accept their explanation. To the extent that they see the Catholic priest as the legitimate authority, they will believe the Christian theological viewpoint. That is what we mean when we say that the Orphan receives a religious initiation alongside the psychic metamorphosis. There is, in essence, a dual metamorphosis at the higher esoteric; one that is a personal experience and one that ties that personal experience to a wider framework of understanding.

To summarise, the metamorphosis that occurs at the higher esoteric at the beginning of the Orphan phase of life consists of the psychic birth of the ego that occurs in the individual and the religious initiation whose purpose is to convey the belief structure of the culture to the Orphan. In the modern West, we replaced the Christian religion, which used to be responsible for the bulk of education, with the technocracy. Thus, modern state-sponsored education became the primary religious institution by which the technocracy communicates the higher esoteric belief structure to the Orphans of society. Our *religious initiation* occurs in school. But every culture has its own exoteric institutions which induct individuals into the higher esoteric belief structures. Moreover, every culture initiates its Orphans around the same time, shortly after the biological metamorphosis of puberty and the psychic metamorphosis that accompanies it.

Conclusion

We have covered a lot of territory in this section, and it is worth recapping so that we don't lose sight of the bigger picture. What the Orphan archetype signifies is the beginning of our character formation in the sexual, economic, political, military, and religious realms. For each of these realms, we can differentiate between the exoteric and the esoteric. We have just seen that religious initiation is the exoteric counterpart to the esoteric metamorphosis that the Orphan goes through. The same is true of the other domains of identity. We may receive training that develops our military skills. These are exoteric to the extent that we can carry them out with the required degree of proficiency, which is recognised by society. But the esoteric element of the training comes only when we have learned the virtues of the good soldier: courage, valour, and patriotism. Similarly, in the political and economic spheres, we exercise our exoteric actions as required, but these only resonate esoterically to the extent that we have dealt with the issues of justice, fairness, and the exercise of power. The metamorphosis that initiates each of these identities can be seen as having both an exoteric and an esoteric component. The exoteric is more straightforward to understand since it comes with official induction into an institution of society, which is normally achieved through a rite of passage. The development of the corresponding esoteric qualities of each identity is less definitive. This difference between the exoteric and esoteric sides of the archetypal metamorphoses will be a recurring theme of our analysis, and we will have an in-depth case study on its particular impact on the Orphan archetype in the second half of the book.

Putting all of this together, we can now map each of these components of character onto our diagram as follows:-

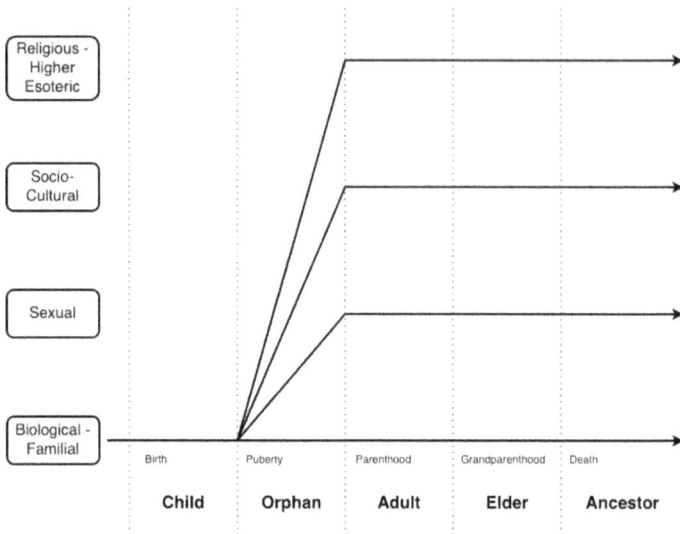

The Orphan archetype is the bridge between the Child and the Adult. It is the time of initiation, training, and education that leads to our mature Adult identity. Let's now proceed to an analysis of the Adult archetype.

The Adult Archetype

Having done most of the heavy lifting in the last section in relation to fleshing out what each domain of identity means, the Adult archetype needs little further elaboration since it represents the culmination of identity formation that begins in the Orphan phase of life. The Adult period sees the full flowering of our character across all the domains of identity. It is the time when we are most active and most productive. If the Orphan is about initiation, training, and education, the Adult is about discipline and willpower as we exercise our capacities to the fullest extent. Most societies recognise this difference by bestowing the full range of rights and responsibilities on the Adult. This is true across all the spheres of identity. Thus, the transitions from Orphan to Adult include those from apprentice to journeyman, student to graduate, single to married, childless to parent, initiate to citizen, etc. All of this is straightforward and needs no further elaboration.

There are two main areas that are less obvious and that we will spend some time exploring. The first relates to the biological-familial domain and the second to the socio-cultural one. Both, however, relate back to the metamorphosis-stability pattern that is the theme of this chapter.

Biological-Familial Identity

Back in our discussion of the Child archetype, we provided a justification for unifying the biological and familial into a single strand of identity on the basis that the Child's development occurs in both domains and that the family exists for the propagation of biological relationships. That same argument applies to the Adult archetype, which, in the domain of the family, requires a transition to Husband-Wife and Father-Mother, the former terms relating to the family and the latter terms to the biological relationship to the Child. In terms of the metamorphosis-stability pattern, the transition to Husband and Wife is achieved via the socio-cultural metamorphosis called *marriage*, while the transition to Mother and Father requires a biological metamorphosis. Therein lies a crucial sexual asymmetry that we have already touched on but which we are now ready to investigate in more depth.

The asymmetry in question is born out of the fact that, although the family is predicated on biological relationships, there can be a difference between what we might call the *social family* and the *biological family*. One example of this is adoption, where children who are not biological relations are brought into the family unit. A second example is one of the oldest stories known to man, which is marital infidelity. It is here that we find a sexual asymmetry at the biological level of being.

For all of history prior to modern science, maternity has always been known with certainty for the very obvious reason that it is the woman who carries the Child. Paternity, on the other hand, has had some level of doubt associated with it, and this is why marital infidelity can result in a baby who is not biologically related to the father. This ancient source of conflict takes on a new importance when we analyse it from within our archetypal model because what it actually means is that there is no biological metamorphosis that marks the Adult period of life for men. The metamorphosis is the same for both sexes in relation to the Child (birth) and Orphan (puberty). However, for the Adult and Elder archetypes, it is only women who have a biological metamorphosis that ushers in the beginning of the phase. The Adult (Parent) phase of life begins with pregnancy and the birth of the Child. That is a biological metamorphosis for the mother only. Similarly, the Elder phase of life for women begins with the biological metamorphosis of menopause. The sexual asymmetry we see is that the Adult and Elder archetypal phases of life have a definitive basis in biology for women, which men lack.

This asymmetry has been pointed out by modern feminists, beginning at least as early as Simone de Beauvoir in her book *The Second Sex*. The focus of feminism ever since has been on what we are calling the socio-cultural domain of identity. Feminists have emphasised the fact that women have been denied access to the economic, political, legal, and military institutions of society. What has gotten little, if any, attention is the fact that the imbalance in the socio-cultural sphere mirrors an imbalance in the biological. In relation to the family and questions of parenthood, men have no biological metamorphosis that ties them to the Parent archetype.

Why is this important? Well, we know that the metamorphoses between the archetypal phases are some of the most difficult times in life. They are difficult because they entail a reconfiguration of one's character across all the dimensions of identity. In relation to the Parent role specifically, that reconfiguration of character involves giving up the relative freedom of the Orphan phase of life for the responsibility of becoming a Parent. Because of the inherent difficulty involved, it is natural that some individuals will try to avoid the metamorphosis. This is true even when the metamorphosis occurs at the biological level of being. It is usually not possible to avoid the biological metamorphosis itself, but it is possible to dissociate from it, often leading to various psychological issues.

Sometimes, it is possible to try and avoid the biological metamorphosis. We know from history and anthropological research that there have always been ways for women to avoid the Parent metamorphosis. We need not go into the gruesome details here because we see the same dynamic in our time play out through the relatively less gruesome technological breakthroughs brought by modern science. The modern debate over abortion can be translated into our archetypal terminology by noting that it gives women the option of avoiding the biological metamorphosis of childbirth and therefore the transition into the Parent role. That option has now become normalised in most Western nations. Meanwhile, we have only recently seen the pattern extended to allowing surgical and pharmaceutical interventions to try and avoid or delay puberty, i.e., the biological metamorphosis that begins the Orphan archetype. There is much that could be said about both of these issues, but we simply note that they imply that some individuals have a very strong desire to avoid these biological metamorphoses and will even undergo risky interventions to do so.

If people are prepared to try to avoid biological metamorphoses, with all the difficulties and risks entailed therein, then it is obvious that individuals will try the same trick if the risk is reduced. This brings us back to the question of paternity. Imagine a society where marriage did not exist and where modern scientific testing could not establish paternity. A man and a woman have sex, and the woman falls pregnant. She tells the man he is the father, but the man does not want to accept the responsibility of becoming a Parent. He has the option to try to escape that metamorphosis by claiming that he is not the biological father, something which can't be proven one way or another in societies without modern science.

Now, in the normal course of events, the man who tried such a trick could face significant social consequences, and the denial of paternity could cause a great deal of societal trouble, which, in less civilised times and with smaller social groupings, could even be an existential threat to the collective. What could a society do to avoid such a potentially disastrous scenario? Well, one way would be to ensure that childbirth always occurs among couples who have already pledged allegiance and faithfulness to one another; in other words, marriage. This wouldn't prevent the possibility of infidelity, but it would stop the man from using that possibility as an excuse to try to weasel out of the metamorphosis required of him to become a Parent.

Thus, we can think of marriage as a socio-cultural metamorphosis that creates the family in advance and therefore solves the potential problem arising from the biological asymmetry between the sexes. The socio-cultural realm is used to correct for an imbalance in the biological one. Could it be that feminists have got the story the wrong way around? What seems like a bias towards men could just as easily be framed as a way to place the legal and economic burden on males in order to bind them to the family and dissuade them from the temptation to back out of the Parent role. To make up for the fact that men lack a biological metamorphosis, society imposes one of its own.

Putting all this together, we see yet another reason to combine the biological and familial domains. Women have the biological metamorphosis of childbirth, which signifies beyond doubt that they have now arrived at the Adult archetype. Since men are lacking at the biological level, they are given a metamorphosis at the socio-cultural level that amounts to a legal, political, economic, and even religious change of archetype. Marriage brings together the biological and familial. Through the institution of the family, the biological metamorphosis of childbirth is shared by both Mother and Father. It ensures their dual transition to the Adult (Parent) archetype with the attendant responsibility of care to the newborn, whether that be the direct physical care usually associated with the Mother, or the indirect economic care usually associated with the Father. In this way, we have a dual metamorphosis that signals the beginning of the Adult phase in the biological-familial domain for both men and women.

Socio-Cultural Identity

Although not everybody will marry and have children, the Husband-Wife and Mother-Father roles are universal across cultures and the norm within them. These metamorphoses in the biological-familial domain are relevant to all members of society as markers of the beginning of the Adult phase of life. In the socio-cultural and religious domains, however, there is a separate kind of metamorphosis for the Adult archetype that also seems to be universal across cultures. To discuss it, we need to introduce a distinction between the

Everyman and what we can broadly call the Elites. The Elites can be further divided into a set of archetypes that map to each of the domains of identity we have described. Thus, we have the Ruler archetype (politics), the Warrior archetype (military and economy), and the Sage archetype (higher esoteric). These are the kings, presidents, prime ministers, generals, CEOs, popes, bishops, philosophers, and scientists. They are the leaders in their respective domains. The Everyman, by contrast, makes up the body of the institutions in those domains. They are the soldiers in the military, the congregation in the church, and the general public in the political system.

Why these distinctions are important for archetypology is because the elites have an extra metamorphosis to go through, one that earns them membership in the elite category. Everybody has the potential to go through the Father-Mother metamorphosis, but only a small group of society will experience the elite metamorphosis. This fact is borne out by the anthropological scholarship, which shows that even small and decentralised cultures have elites. It's also true that elite metamorphosis forms the basis of some of the most famous myths, legends, and stories from ancient and modern sources. To take just one famous example from modern film, Luke Skywalker goes through elite initiation in the original *Star Wars* trilogy, as signified by his receiving instruction from two teachers, Obi-Wan Kenobi and Yoda. The other members of the group, such as Hans Solo and Chewbacca, do not go through such an initiation, and we would call them Everyman archetypes for that reason.

Although it goes against the democratic and egalitarian ideals of the modern West, every society has elites. The pathway to elite membership is either fixed at birth due to descent or is determined during the Orphan period of life. In both cases, however, there is a special form of education and training set aside for membership in the elite class. The easiest way for us to understand that in the modern world is to think of professional sports. Nobody would deny that a professional sports player receives a higher standard of training than a weekend warrior. The same is also obviously true of the military, where special forces receive a longer and more rigorous form of training than the general soldiery. In relation to the Sage archetype, every religion has a special form of initiation for esoteric practitioners (priests, monks, nuns, etc.). In our modern technocratic society, the PhD demarcates the true "expert" from the rest of the educated masses. We can find direct counterparts for each of these modern elites in the anthropological and historical literature.

The purpose of elite initiation is to provoke a metamorphosis in the initiate which leads to the kind of exceptional performance that is expected. We can capture the difference between this form of initiation and the one given to the general public by adapting a concept used by William James, which he subsequently modified from the teachings of Jesus. James distinguished between the *once born* and the *twice born*. The general public, represented by the Everyman archetype, are the once born. In James' definition, they accept the underlying belief structures of their society without question. The form of initiation given to members of the general public during the Orphan phase of life has as its primary purpose to induct them into the belief structures of society, not to question or criticise those structures.

Elite education is different. It is designed to make the individual *twice born*, which requires them to call into question the belief structures in order to be able to fully understand them. This is not just an exercise in philosophising, although that is a perfectly legitimate form of training for the Sage archetype. Elite performance is predicated on failure, or at least the risk of failure. It implies being taken beyond the limits of what one thought was possible, whether that be in the physical domain, as for military and sports elites; in the economic and political domain, as for rulers of nations; or in the theological and philosophical domains, as for the great sages. To achieve a truly elite standard, even in a field that is mostly about physical performance, requires one to break through all kinds of mental barriers and to challenge one's preconceived notions. This implies a higher esoteric and sometimes also a biological metamorphosis. Thus, we can say that the true attainment of elite performance is predicated on a metamorphosis.

Yet again, we must remember our distinction between the exoteric and the esoteric here. The true attainment of elite performance is always esoteric in nature in that it pertains to the individual. What the anthropological literature shows, however, is that every society confers elite status via a series of exoteric markers that differentiate the elites from the general public. These markers include special forms of address, special clothing, restricted access often enforced with the threat of violence, and geographical separation. The king in his castle, wearing his crown, and being addressed as *his majesty* is one of the more conspicuous forms of exoteric status marking. But any time this combination of properties exists, you are dealing with an elite class. Yes, that very much includes doctors, scientists, and other members of the modern technocratic elite in Western society. The white lab coat and "Dr." form of address are every bit as powerful in our time as the priest's robes were in times past.

As is always the case in human affairs, the exoteric and the esoteric can get out of alignment. The most common form of this in relation to the elite class of society is what we generally call *corruption*. Within our model, this is the situation where those who are not esoterically fit for a role get promoted to the exoteric position that exists for that role. This is a very common story from history with its tales of mad kings, crazy emperors, evil priests, and the like. We can further subdivide corruption into plain old incompetence. This is the scenario where a person who does not have the requisite skills, knowledge, or experience gets promoted to a position of authority, usually through nepotism. A second form of corruption is the competent practitioner who uses their position for personal gain rather than public service.

There is a rarer form of mismatch between the exoteric and esoteric dimensions of the elite class, and that is where there is an oversupply of those who are esoterically capable relative to the number of exoteric positions available. This is arguably the case in the modern West, where universal education has made possible the growth in the number of those who have, at least in theory, attained elite initiation. In truth, this is part of a larger problem with the hierarchical institutions of civilisation, which must always allow only a small number to ascend to the top of the tree and which therefore cannot always offer roles to those who are fit and ready for them.

Although the training for elite performance usually begins during the Orphan phase of life, it is not possible to know who will actually attain and demonstrate it until the Adult phase. For this reason, we will add the elite distinction into the Adult archetype on our diagram as follows:-

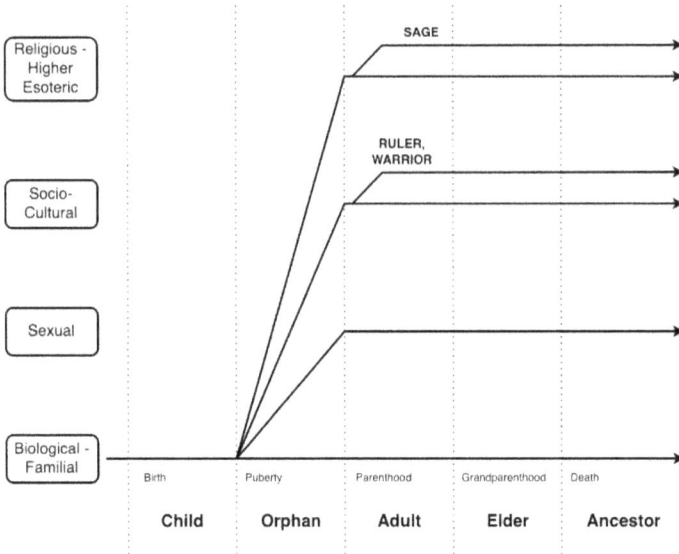

Putting it all together, we see that the Adult phase of life represents the full expression of our character across multiple fields of identity. It is the time when we are most capable and productive. We are able to call on the qualities of determination, willpower, and discipline to the fullest extent, and we do this across familial, economic, political, military, and religious domains. That is the positive side of the equation, but it's equally possible that we may slip into shadow forms during this time. The shadow forms for elite practitioners normally revolve around the temptation of corruption that always comes with the attainment of power. Having learned the rules of the game, one can get away with abusing them, often for very long periods of time. Hence, the constant flow of scandals that emanate from on high. For the Everyman, corruption takes the form not of an abuse of power but of a dissipation into pleasure. William James noted that the *once born* are more able than the *twice born* to enjoy the simple joys of life, but the temptation is to indulge to excess. Therefore, addiction is the primary risk for the Everyman, whether in alcohol, drugs, entertainment, gluttony, or sloth.

The distinction between elites and the general public also manifests in the appearance of certain pathologies in the broader social matrix. The Every-man provides a necessary common-sense counterweight to the intellectual pretensions of the elite classes. Where too much power accrues to the elites, we find the pursuit of absurd ideological schemes disconnected from reality or brutal military dictatorships that pilfer from the public purse. Meanwhile, too much power in the hands of the general public leads to petty corruption, such as is demonstrated in Aristophanes' great comedy *The Wasps*, which we mention purely to show that this problem has been around for a very long time and will no doubt remain a feature of human affairs in perpetuity.

To the Adult phase of life belongs all the joys and trials of being a parent, of the workplace or economic sphere, and of political and religious engagement. The theme which shines forth most strongly for this archetype is willpower, whether one wills what is good or what is bad. It is the relinquishing of this willpower which forms the primary difficulty that initiates the final phase of life. Let us now turn to the last of our four primary archetypes.

The Elder Archetype

Although we have been at pains to point out that the metamorphoses that initiate the Orphan and Adult phases of life need to be understood as resonating across all three major components of character, it is also true that the emphasis for these two archetypes is on the socio-cultural in just the same way that the emphasis for the Child archetype is on the biological. In the Orphan and early Adult phases of life, we are junior and inexperienced. Our mission is to find a place in society and establish ourselves. The socio-cultural aspects of identity dominate so much during this time that there is a risk that the individual becomes lost in a conformity to social convention that extinguishes individual thought and action.

By contrast, the metamorphosis that ushers in the Elder phase of life resonates primarily at the higher esoteric level of being. Jung called this time of life the "confrontation with the soul.". If it is the ego which bursts forth at the beginning of the Orphan archetype, then it should be the soul which makes its appearance at the beginning of the Elder. Now, just as the psychic birth of the ego corresponds with the biological metamorphosis of puberty, the confrontation with the soul correlates in women with the onset of menopause. As we have already stated, men do not have a dramatic enough biological change that we would call it a metamorphosis, but it is true that a number of changes take place at this time, the most important of which is a decline in testosterone. Meanwhile, women see a relative rise in testosterone and a fall in oestrogen. These hormonal reversals map directly to Jung's claim that the soul takes the opposite gender to biology. Thus, the man must confront his feminine *anima* and the woman her masculine *animus*.

Perhaps the primary change of perspective which may usher in the Elder phase of life is the recognition that one has a finite amount of time remaining in the world. The Child and Orphan phases have a timelessness to them, which forms a large part of their charm. Life seems as if it will go on forever. Meanwhile, the Adult years are about taking care of business, knuckling down and getting the job done, and whatever other metaphors we may use to signify the discipline and determination that mark this most productive time of life. The Orphan and Adult phases are also about following orders since one is necessarily in a junior position in the social hierarchy.

It is partly as a by-product of experience that the finitude of life comes into view. The idealism of youth gives way to the pragmatism of adulthood as one learns the difference between having an idea and implementing it. Only when one has achieved something multiple times does one know what ingredients are required for its attainment, including sometimes more than a dash of luck. The pain of failure comes to be represented as if it were "lost time". The Adult phase of life also shifts into the Elder once we learn the difference between doing things because social convention requires us to and doing things because we actually value them in themselves. If the active use of willpower is one of the defining features of the Adult phase of life, it is also true that one realises that many of the things one willed were not actually the things one really wanted. That follows from the fact that one was just taking orders as befits a junior place in the social hierarchy.

Thus, the Elder archetype begins with the dual realisation of the finitude of life and the desire not to waste one's time on things that are of no value. Both of these may sound like a positive development, but in actual fact, they set the individual on a collision course with their society. The things that are of no value to you are nevertheless of value to your society since it was by following the orders of society that you came to be involved in them. For you to say that you now have your own values that you want to work towards implies a contradiction with your society, or at least certain sections of it. Thus, the assertion of one's own values brings necessary social conflict. This is not the kind of social conflict that comes out of membership in a specific group of society, such as a political party or a football team, who are always necessarily competing with each other. Rather, it is the conflict of one's individuality against society in general.

The reason why this is such a challenge is not just because it requires us to stand by the courage of our convictions; it is also because we can be held responsible for those convictions. During the Orphan and Adult periods of life, we do our duty. We are governed by social necessity, and one of the nice things about that is that we get to offload responsibility onto those who give us our orders. To assert one's own value system and to act by it is to take responsibility for the outcomes of our actions. The Elder has the freedom of choice. But when we make genuine choices, we reveal our values. That can be just as much of a shock to ourselves as to others. The Elder who takes their accumulated wealth from a lifetime of disciplined work and squanders it in the pursuit of pleasure is revealing that they value pleasure above all else. The realisation of that can cause significant cognitive dissonance since it brings into question our actions from earlier in life. If it is the pursuit of pleasure that we value above all else, what was the point of all that disciplined work? Was it all a waste of time during which we could have been having fun? That is why we say that the Elder phase of life is a confrontation with the higher esoteric. It is the old philosophical question of the meaning of life, not as an abstract and bloodless scholarly issue, but as a real reckoning with our conscience.

If we zoom out from these specific issues, what is really going on with the Elder archetype is the confrontation with death. Theologians and philosophers from time immemorial have known that death forces us to confront the issue of meaning most forcefully. As the Elder phase of life goes on, death comes closer, and the philosophical and theological questions become harder to ignore. The confrontation with death may seem to be a very personal experience since it is the individual who must face it directly. But our understanding of the meaning of death comes from the wider culture in which we live. We noted earlier that the Orphan phase of life is the time of psychic birth and that this psychic birth is explained according to the metaphysics of the culture in question. The prospect of physical death makes those metaphysical questions far more immediate because the understanding of what happens at death is contained in those cultural scripts. Those scripts will not just be followed by the Elder facing death but also by the family, friends, and wider society. Death is not just a personal issue but a social one. It is a personal and collective confrontation with the higher esoteric.

From an archetypal point of view, we can represent these issues by noting that there are two archetypes that come after the Elder and which therefore apply to us after we are dead. The first is the Ancestor and the second is the Gods/Spirits. The latter of these is practically a synonym for the higher esoteric since it pertains to the deepest metaphysical beliefs of a culture. It is no secret that the modern West no longer believes in this archetype. We have replaced it with something else. Since this represents our highest beliefs, it also, by default, implies an understanding of the meaning of death and therefore has a major impact during the Elder phase of life. It is no coincidence that this is why the Elder archetype has become highly problematic for us.

To understand why, we need to explore the implications of modern Western metaphysics and how they create such difficulty for the Elder archetype's confrontation with death. We're going to approach this topic in a way that might initially seem unrelated but should become clear as we go. It will also become important later in the book. Let's talk about stories.

History vs Story

In relation to our post-death archetypes, modern Western culture would say that stories about the Ancestors are "history", while stories about the Gods/Spirits are either theology if you are a believer or fiction if you are not. In any case, we make a strong division between history (fact) and story (fiction). However, this distinction is nowhere near as clean-cut as we think it is.

The English words *story* and *history* both come from the Latin *historia.* To this day, almost all European languages use the word *historia* to denote both story (fiction) and history (fact), while modern German also combines both meanings into a single word - *geschichte.* What this etymology reveals is that our modern hard distinction between history-as-fact and story-as-fiction was not shared by our forebears. There were practical reasons why this was the case.

For most of history, most people have been illiterate, and the main form of storytelling was oral. There was little to no tradition of writing down facts with the intention of verifying them or with the notion that they would remain truths over time. In this cultural and societal setting, story and history were much the same thing. To choose a more neutral term, let's call them narratives. A narrative has a hero. It was obvious to the audience of a narrative whether the hero was alive, deceased in living memory, or deceased at some unknown time in the past. Most importantly, the difference between a completely fictional hero and one who was deceased at an unknown time in the past was minimal since there was no way to verify facts about the latter anyway.

Thus, narratives featuring a hero who is *deceased in living memory* are about Ancestors, while it is the Gods/Spirits who are *deceased at an unknown time in the past.* For most of history, the difference between these two states was determined by the normal human lifespan. Once all the people who knew the hero of the story from first-hand experience were dead, the story became about Gods/Spirits. Even in Roman times, when the culture had far less of a historical consciousness than we have, a monumental figure such as Julius Caesar quickly ceased to be an Ancestor and became a god. This happened within just a couple of generations. Meanwhile, most of the great myths from history, which we give the status of being primarily "fiction", are about figures who were almost certainly real people at one time. This is true of the *Epic of Gilgamesh*, most of the Greek myths that we still study, and the Bible.

In fact, our modern approach to history owes a great deal to the centuries of work spent studying the Bible. In particular, it was in the 19th century that a strong division began to be made between Bible stories that were factually true (history) versus mythically true (fiction). This helped to create what we still believe to be a firm distinction between truth and fiction. History became concerned with the truth; stories and myths became products of the imagination. The result was to both demythologise history, which became concerned solely with the accumulation of verifiable facts, and trivialise fiction, which was relegated to the domain of entertainment and amusement.

There were two notable reactions against these developments. The first was in the scholarly domain of history, where, against the notion of history as a mere collection of facts, there arose the idea of history as a repeating cycle. This came to be known as comparative history. This trend represented a re-mythologising. It put the story back into history. The meaning of this will become clearer in the second half of the book when we conduct an in-depth analysis of stories.

A subtly different kind of re-mythologising came via the Jungian approach to myth as a repository of archetypes. Rather than consigning stories, myths, and literature to the domain of entertainment, Jung reconnected them with the deeper truths of the psyche. Stories were now seen to be full of archetypes, and archetypes lived in the collective unconscious. Therefore, stories were once again about the eternal truths, now revealed by the contents of the unconscious mind.

What we are calling Gods/Spirits is very similar to what Jung meant by the archetypes of the collective unconscious. If we use Julius Caesar as the example yet again, his transition from Ancestor, who people directly remembered as a real human being, to a God/Spirit is the transition from the conscious mind to the Jungian unconscious. Having descended into the unconscious, Caesar becomes an archetype synonymous with the Ruler and/or Warrior in the same way that Jesus or Socrates have become the Sage archetype. As archetypes of the unconscious, specific facts about their lives become unimportant. What is important is what we might more generally call their *spirit*, hence our use of Gods/Spirits as a name for the general archetype that is at play.

It follows from this that the modern Western distinction between history (fact) and story (fiction) is also the distinction between the conscious and unconscious minds. Since the archetypes live in the collective unconscious, our desire to demythologise history and turn it into a series of facts is the desire to pull it out of the unconscious and bring it to consciousness. This prevents Caesar from becoming an archetype and turns him instead into a historical individual. This is no accidental or arbitrary occurrence. It follows quite specifically from our beliefs about the higher esoteric. The desire for facts, history, and consciousness reveals that we value "truth" above all else. That word has become problematic for us nowadays, but back at the beginning of the Enlightenment, it really did represent a new belief structure, a new conception of the higher esoteric.

Part of the reason why there was a backlash against the Enlightenment ideals was because the desire for facts implicitly denied the infinite or eternal. To the extent that the Gods/Spirits belong to the infinite world, they exist indefinitely. The loss of the infinite brings us down to a finite world of past and future. The Ancestors belong to the past and the Children to the future. As long as the past is seen to guarantee the future, then this chain can remain unbroken. But a severance in the chain replaces the backward-looking connection to the Ancestors with a forward-looking utopianism in which youth takes pride of place. The modern West has a peculiar version of this severance with the past because our scientific mentality has turned the past into a set of facts, which has inadvertently had the effect of turning it into a battleground for ideological warfare. Since no fact exists without an ideology to justify it, history has become a divisive enterprise between competing ideological groups rather than the implicitly unifying act of myth-making. Ironically, "science" in the form of science fiction has stepped in to fill the void, becoming one of our primary myth-making devices because it opens outward into the unknown of the future, unlike the past, which has become mired in "facts". We can no longer dream about the past, but we can dream about the future.

The reason why all this matters is because, although very few of us will attain the stature and importance of a Caesar, the beliefs our society has about the higher esoteric govern our own transition from Elder to Ancestor and then to God/Spirit. When we say that the Elder phase of life is the confrontation with death, it is also about how we as individuals think about our death and how those closest to us and our society understand it too. The funeral rites and grieving process of a culture are a direct reflection of its understanding of the higher esoteric. One of the main ways that manifests is in the form of stories. But if the story of an Ancestor is about history, then it is reduced to dry facts that cannot possibly capture anything about the individual that we hold truly dear. On the other hand, stories not based in fact have been implicitly relegated to the domain of fiction. At best, they are just personal beliefs or experiences, fleeting in nature and with no larger meaning or purpose. What is denied is the transition of the individual to the infinite realm.

All of this follows from modern Western culture's denial of the archetype of God/Spirit. Nietzsche's *death of God* reverberates back through the archetypes of Ancestor and Elder. What is usually thought of as an abstract philosophical question becomes very real when the time comes to grieve the death of the Elder, and it is clear that our society has a major problem with the grieving process. The Canadian author, Stephen Jenkinson, has most eloquently outlined these problems in several of his books based on his lived experience as a grief counsellor. In short, we have forgotten how to grieve. We have done so because our scientific conception of the higher esoteric is not adapted to the grieving process. In some sense, it is a denial of it. In the modern West, we now face the Elder phase of life against this cultural background, and this has made the confrontation with death far more anxiety-ridden for us than it has been for most cultures throughout history. The loss of the Elder role in our society is certainly partly related to these developments. We inherently shy away from the problem and pretend it doesn't exist.

Nevertheless, death is inevitable. As always, the biological domain marches on irrespective of our wishes. The Elder phase of life is still the confrontation with the higher esoteric. The progression of the archetypes must still be navigated. What has changed is our conception of that progression, which has moved from this:

God/Spirits (via Myth)				
				Ancestor
			Elder	
		Adult/ Parent		
	Orphan			
Child				

To this:-

Science/History (via Ideology)				
				Ancestor
			Elder	
		Adult/ Parent		
	Orphan			
Child				

Science, history, and ideology are every bit as esoteric as the myths and legends they have replaced. But this new conception of the higher esoteric has left a void. If we remember back to our earlier notion that the Sage archetype is the one who is responsible for the guardianship of a culture's understanding of the higher esoteric, for the best part of a millennium, modern Western culture had as its Sage archetype the practitioners of the Christian religion: priest, bishop, and pope. The average person's confrontation with the higher esoteric was done within the structure and belief system of that religion. That structure has now been largely replaced by the Enlightenment model whereby our Sage archetypes are technocrats backed by "science". Whereas once upon a time it would have been a priest who was called to conduct the rites of death, it is now a doctor or nurse who accompanies us in our final hours. Nine out of ten people now die either in a hospital or a nursing home, surrounded by the technocracy (medical professionals). Although we don't think of them that way, and they don't think of themselves that way, the truth is that they are our Sages and they represent our conception of the higher esoteric. But our technocrats are not trained, and don't see it as their job, to manage the grieving process. That is why we are left without guidance while navigating the final archetypal transition of our lives.

Of course, these issues are specific to modern Western culture. The reason we have had to go into such depth about them is because the Elder has almost disappeared from our society. This is a theme we'll be talking about throughout the book, but it has been necessary to introduce it here to prove to a Western readership that the Elder really does exist and not just as a character in fantasy movies.

The death of the Elder is the completion of the full life's journey. It is naturally a summation of that journey and reflection on its meaning. In every culture, the Elder's confrontation with death is the broader society's confrontation with the higher esoteric. The death of the Elder is a challenge to the higher esoteric belief structures and is therefore a metamorphosis not just for the individual but for all those who bear witness. For all the other archetypes we have looked at, the biological metamorphosis comes at the beginning of the archetypal phase. The paradox of the Elder is that the metamorphosis which triggers the confrontation with the higher esoteric comes at the end. The Elder is called on to affirm their values both in their own lifetime and with a view to the time after their death. The reason why stories are relevant here is because, in some small sense, the Elder gets to write the story of their own death and what occurs thereafter. Another way to think about the metamorphosis that ushers in the confrontation with the higher esoteric is that it's the time when we decide to start writing that story.

Conclusion

We have covered a lot of ground in this chapter, and it is worth concluding with a summary of the main properties of each archetype. We began by stating that the archetypes can be broken up into metamorphosis and stability phases. The metamorphosis is the difficult transition period that ushers in the archetype. It tends to last several years as we come to grips with the biological, socio-cultural, and higher esoteric changes thrust upon us. Once we have dealt with the difficulty of reconfiguring our identity, we then enter the long stable period of the archetype, which comes with its own difficulties and challenges.

It makes sense, then, to summarise the archetypes according to the major properties of the metamorphosis and the stability periods. Beginning with the former, we can present the key features of the metamorphosis in table form as follows:-

	Biological-Familial	Socio-Cultural	Higher Esoteric
Child	Birth	N/A	N/A
Orphan	Puberty – Parental conflict	Initiation	Psychic birth of the ego
Adult	Marriage-Childbirth	Graduation to Everyman or Elite	Acceptance of responsibility
Elder	Menopause – Birth of grandchildren	Mentor, teacher, guide	Confrontation with the higher esoteric

The metamorphosis period for the Child is almost entirely about the biological challenges of birth and the dangerous period thereafter. There is no socio-cultural or higher esoteric challenge to speak of. But the Child does need to form a bond with its Parents, although this is almost entirely in the hands of the latter, and therefore not an adaptation the Child must make.

The Orphan metamorphosis resonates across all domains of identity, with puberty in the biological sphere, the birth of the ego in the higher esoteric, and the initiation into the institutions of society in the socio-cultural. Not only is the period difficult due to the range of new experiences encountered, but there is also the loss of the pleasant features of childhood, such as playfulness and lack of responsibility.

For most people, the most important Adult metamorphosis is marriage and the arrival of children. Both of these entail a major change of lifestyle and the require the establishment of a stable equilibrium in the household. In the socio-cultural domain, we graduate to full membership of the institutions of society to which we belong, with the extra responsibility entailed. At the higher esoteric, the main challenge is the acceptance of that extra responsibility, as we must now bear both in the familial and socio-cultural domains.

For the Elder, the arrival of grandchildren is the metamorphosis in the familial domain that begins this archetype. In the socio-cultural, there is a transition towards more of a mentoring, teaching, and leadership role. Finally, we spent most of our discussion talking about the difficult confrontation with the higher esoteric that occurs at the higher esoteric. The unifying thread of all of these is the march of time and the approach of death.

All of the events in the above table can be seen as causing major state changes that usher in the new archetype. Combined, they force a complete re-evaluation of our identity. The interaction between the various elements is a large contributor to the overall difficulty of the metamorphosis period. As we will see later in the book, problems in one area can easily magnify into general issues that threaten our whole being. As we will also see later in the book, every society has a set of social scripts which demarcate these major changes and thereby assist both the individual and the society to work through them. The universality of such practices speaks to the recognition that metamorphosis is a period of heightened danger.

Once the danger period is over, we get into the stability part of the archetype, which we can summarise as follows:-

	Biological-Familial	Socio-Cultural	Higher Esoteric
Child	Growth of Child's body	Basic initiation into society	Imagination and play
Orphan	Growth of Adult body	Education and training	Learning to manage the ego
Adult	Raising of children	Full contribution and responsibility	Full expression of will
Elder	Aging - Grandparenthood	Teaching the next generation	Incorporation of soul

Another way to think about the stability period is that it is the time when we must accomplish whatever *mission* the archetype has for us. For the Child, the continued growth of the body as well as learning how to use it is key in the biological domain. There is usually a basic level of initiation into society and the subsequent development of social skills which comes with it. At the higher esoteric, the exercise of imagination and play can be seen as a precursor to the more advanced faculties that come later.

For the Orphan, the mission is to begin the transition towards adulthood. There is the onset of the Adult's body, including sexual maturity. In the socio-cultural sphere, there is a period of education and training to learn the skills that are needed for mature identity. In the higher esoteric, there is the need to learn to control the ego. This is also the onset of what the medieval period called the *age of reason*. Thus, the education and training also imply the ability to think about problems in a more abstract sense. This is behind the idealism that we often associate with this period of life.

Adulthood is all about responsibility. In the familial domain, it is about raising children. In the socio-cultural domain, it is about contributing to the institutions that we are now full members of. In the higher esoteric domain, all of this can be summarised by the exercise of will, with its associated properties of determination and resolve.

We know that the Elder archetype must confront the higher questions of meaning and purpose. A way that this occurs, which we will explore more in the next chapter, is through taking up positions of mentorship and guidance. This is done in the familial domain through the role of the grandparent, while in the socio-cultural domain it comes naturally to those with the most experience in any given field.

This focus on the archetypes in isolation is perfectly valid. However, even in our discussion in this chapter, we have seen that each archetype seems to naturally pair with one other. This is most obvious in relation to the Child-Parent pairing, where the Child really is completely dependent on the Parents. What is more interesting and will be more surprising for us in the modern West is that there is an Orphan-Elder pairing which is just as fundamental. As if the metamorphosis period wasn't difficult enough, we're about to see that it is even more problematic since it relies on the archetypal pair also fulfilling their role.

Chapter 3: The Archetypal Pairs

In this chapter we are going to add another property to our model, which both increases the combinatorial complexity and also the qualitative depth of our understanding. Each of our four primary archetypes has a special relationship with one other archetype. Since the archetypal roles are reversed as we progress through life, this amounts to just two primary archetypal pairs of Child-Parent (Adult) and Orphan-Elder. The first of these requires almost no explanation since it is not only a core aspect of our lived experience; it is essentially a tautology. The only way to become a Parent is to have a Child. The only way to be a Child is to have Parents. However, as we have seen several times with our model, what seems simple at first glance often reveals surprising complexity. The Child-Parent relationship is a tautology at the biological level of being but not at the socio-familial and higher esoteric. A biological parent need not fill the socio-familial role of Mother or Father, and neither the biological nor the socio-familial relationship guarantees the feelings of love and affection that we hope exist at the higher esoteric.

Although the Child-Parent pairing is a universal of human culture, the way it manifests can vary greatly across societies. In the West, the nuclear family has become the default model, especially in the post-war years. Although something like this model does seem to be common across cultures, the anthropological literature shows other forms, such as polygamy and nomadic tribal lifestyles, that push the definitional boundaries of the Child-Parent pairing. In fact, as we will see in this chapter, the modern West has ended up with a rather extreme emphasis on the Child-Parent pairing, which has come at the expense of the second pairing: the Orphan-Elder. Just as the Child-

Parent relationship seems self-evidently fundamental to us, the Orphan-Elder has all but disappeared, at least in its exoteric forms. In most cultures, the Orphan-Elder pair would be as conspicuous as the Child-Parent.

From these brief reflections, we can see that the introduction of the archetypal pair concept tends to expand our scope of analysis beyond the individual and more towards the social and cultural aspects of the broader collective. Once we extend our perspective beyond the individual archetype to the archetypal pair, it seems natural to extend even further and view the archetypes in their relation to the society and culture in which they exist. That is what we will do in this chapter. We will see how larger cultural currents place strain on the archetypes and archetypal pairs, leading to counter currents that seem to flow from a kind of archetypal logic. To demonstrate how that works, we will need to take a couple of deep dives into modern Western culture, which will give us a chance to put our model to work as an analytical tool for understanding real-world issues.

We begin, however, on the relatively safe ground of the most fundamental of relationships, the Child-Parent pair.

The Child-Parent Pair

Modern psychology has understandably focused its attention on the individual. This makes sense when we consider that it had its origins in medicine and therefore was primarily concerned with combating mental illness. However, if we think about arguably the most famous concept espoused by the psychoanalysts, Freud's *Oedipus Complex*, we see that it was really about the relationship between individuals. Using our terminology, the Oedipus Complex was about the interaction of three archetypes: Father, Mother, and Child. Furthermore, the complex did not necessarily lead to pathology; rather, it was a challenge to be faced, from which pathology was only one possible outcome. This is the pattern we will pursue in this chapter as we describe the more abstract dynamics that apply to the interaction between the archetypes. For this purpose, we will mostly combine the Mother and Father into a single archetype called the Parent and posit that there exists a Child-Parent pair. The reason to do this is because we are concerned not so much with the lower-level developments in the relationship, such as the Oedipus Complex, but with the overall pattern of metamorphosis-stability that we identified in chapter two.

In relation to the Child-Parent pairing, we have already described the main points of the dynamic. We know that the Child and Mother undergo a simultaneous metamorphosis at the biological level of being (pregnancy and childbirth). We know that the Father misses out on the biological metamorphosis but is included in the socio-cultural metamorphosis of marriage that should precede it. To the extent that marriage is governed by the higher esoteric beliefs of the culture, these constitute a full metamorphosis across all three of our primary domains of identity. In fact, it is clear from these considerations that the institution of marriage and the family is predicated on the Child-Parent archetypal pairing. As we will see later in this chapter, the Orphan-Elder pairing belongs to the socio-cultural institutions of society. Thus, our two archetypal pairs of Child-Parent and Orphan-Elder relate respectively to the two broad categories of identity: the biological-familial and socio-cultural.

When analysing the formation of the archetypal pair, we can capture the metamorphoses required using the following diagram:-

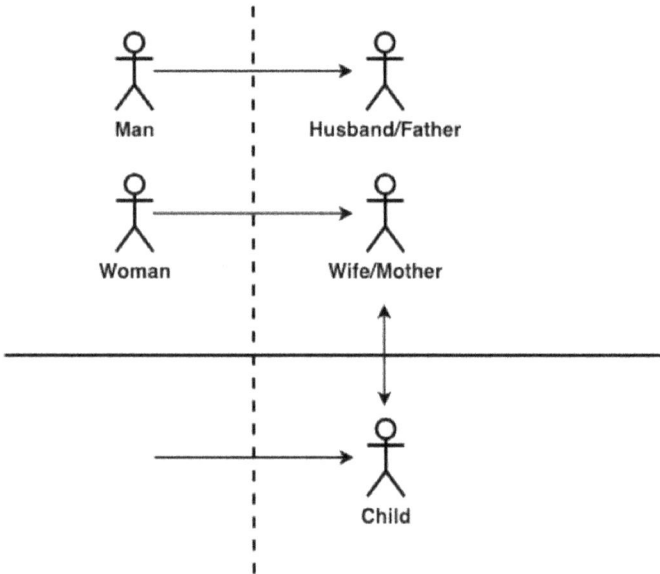

The dotted vertical line represents the archetypal boundary. On the left-hand side of the line is the old archetype that must be transitioned away from, and on the right side is the one which must be transitioned into. Since the Child has no prior archetypal identity (setting aside questions of rebirth, past lives, etc.), the first field is empty for them. The initial state for the Parents will depend on their personal circumstances, but for the first Child we can say that, at least in the biological-familial domain, they manifest the Orphan archetype. They must relinquish that archetype and transition into the Adult (Husband-Wife, Father-Mother).

In reality, the metamorphosis is not an instantaneous transition but a lengthy process. The biological metamorphoses for both Mother and Child last nine months. The courtship, proposal, and marriage planning phases that unite Husband and Wife also typically take place over a relatively long duration. Then there is the difficult period after birth where all members of the family must settle in to a new life. Since the metamorphosis is a long process, we might represent it more accurately on the diagram as follows:-

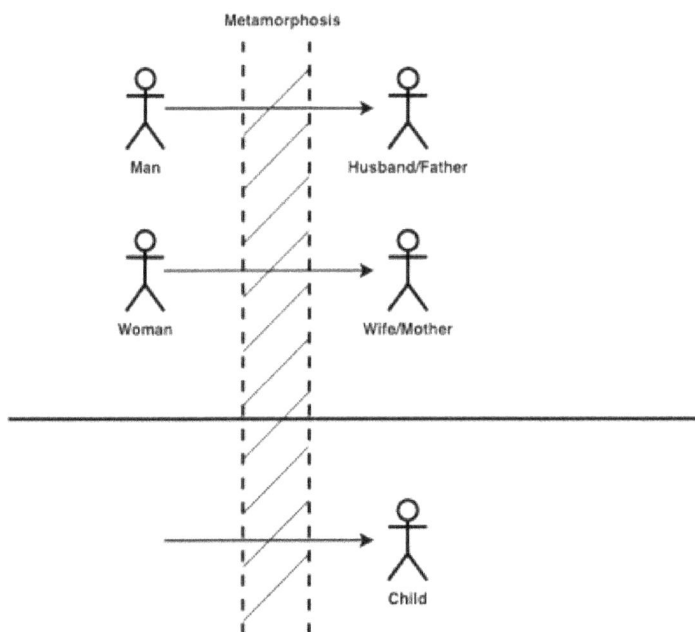

The process is made more complicated by the fact that it is not necessarily synchronous or coordinated across the levels of being. That is, the biological, socio-cultural, and higher esoteric metamorphoses can occur at different times for the individual but also in the interactions between the archetypal pairs. It is because of this uncertainty and instability that the metamorphoses are times of heightened risk for all members.

Since it is only the Mother and Child who go through a biological metamorphosis, the risks in this domain are limited to them. Prior to advances in modern medicine, this risk was significant. Both infant mortality and mortality in mothers due to complications in childbirth were in double-digit percentages. The danger was concentrated in the period on and immediately after childbirth. Even in the modern world, where medical advances have significantly reduced the risk, it is still highest immediately after birth and drops significantly after the first several months. Thus, the metamorphosis period does not just include the dramatic event of childbirth, but also the period of rapid adaptation that occurs thereafter. Eventually, the risk subsides and we move out of metamorphosis. The stability period of the cycle begins for the Child in about the second or third year. For the Mother, it is much earlier.

In addition to these biological risks, there must be a metamorphosis at the familial level to incorporate the Child into a harmonious interaction with other family members. A family that does not settle down into a new routine based around care of the newborn can be in for trouble. Statistics show that divorce is far more likely in the period immediately after the birth of a child when the stresses of the archetypal transition are highest. This relates to potential problems at the higher esoteric for Mother and Father, with Mothers especially at risk from psychological problems in the aftermath of childbirth. Thus, we have biological, socio-cultural, and higher esoteric challenges for all members of the new archetypal pair that must be formed.

But the metamorphosis period is not just about adapting to the new challenges that are thrown up. It is also about letting go of the previous archetype. This is almost never an issue of biology, but of socio-cultural and higher esoteric problems. Since the Child has no prior archetype, there is no issue of letting go of a previous identity. But the Parents must learn to relinquish their identity as Orphans. This amounts to navigating a major change of lifestyle due to the necessity to make care of the Child their first priority. It involves giving up the relative freedom and possibility that comes with the Orphan phase of life. Thus, the challenge that the Parents face is not just related to the new knowledge and skills they must acquire to move into the Parent role, but also to the mental and social challenge of letting go of their pre-parental lives. If the Parents fail that transition, then they are not accepting the responsibility for the care of the Child. In this case, the very existence of the Child can be threatened, and society will hopefully intervene to solve the problem.

What the concept of the archetypal pair makes explicit is that there are simultaneous metamorphoses at play and that problems with the metamorphosis of one party become problems with the other members of the archetypal pair. In relation to the Child-Parent pairing, this is a statement of the obvious. A sick Child is a problem for the Parents. A distressed Mother or absent Father can be a problem for the Child. What is perhaps less obvious is that the way in which each member of the pair experiences any difficulties is determined by the archetype they manifest. The Child resonates primarily at the biological level of being, and any problems with the Parents affect the Child to the extent that they disrupt its biological development. By contrast, the Parents have a fully developed character in all three primary dimensions of identity and may experience sickness or other problems in the Child as feelings of shame, inadequacy, and despair. The issue may also manifest biologically in illness.

Once the dangerous metamorphosis period is over, the archetypal pairing moves into the long stability phase of the cycle. This lasts until the next pairing is ready to be formed. Thus, the Child-Parent relationship remains dominant until the time when the Orphan-Elder takes over. Of course, stability does not imply happiness, virtue, or other positive qualities. As Tolstoy famously wrote, "All happy families are alike; each unhappy family is unhappy in its own way." Once stability is established, even a stability in which the participants are generally unhappy, it tends to hold because the only way to break the stability is to recreate the uncertainty and unpredictability of the metamorphosis period. Most people will subconsciously avoid that if they can and one of the ways to do so is to make the negative traits of the relationship part of one's identity. As psychoanalysis discovered, unravelling those complexes requires an extended process that can last months or even years.

Putting this together, we can extrapolate the following parameters in relation to the archetypal pair concept: 1) each archetype comes with a pair that is its most important relationship; 2) the metamorphosis period includes the formation of the pair relationship; 3) the risk of the metamorphosis is greater because problems with one member of the pair become problems for all members; 4) even after the metamorphosis period is over, if any member of the pair breaks the relationship, all members are forced into a new metamorphosis to re-establish their identity.

There is a fifth point to add, which is that the archetypal pair relationship is strongly affected by the higher esoteric beliefs of the culture. Let's look at an example of that, using recent developments from Western culture.

If we think back to our earlier point about the sexual asymmetry around childbirth whereby the biological metamorphosis that ushers in the Parent archetype for women is lacking for men, we noted that marriage was the corresponding socio-cultural metamorphosis that almost every society sets up to precede childbirth. Marriage is the institution tailored specifically for the Child-Parent pairing. The biological status of that pairing is immutable, at least at the genetic level. Once upon a time in Western civilisation, the socio-cultural status was also immutable. Divorce was almost entirely prohibited, meaning that both the biological and socio-cultural structures built around the Child-Parent relationship could not be broken except by the intervention of external circumstances.

At that time, the higher esoteric belief structure that governed the Child-Parent pairing was set by the Christian church. It is no coincidence then that modern divorce laws were implemented not by Christian Elders but by parliamentary legislation in the 19th century as part of a larger move by the state to disintermediate the church. As we discussed in the last chapter's analysis of the Elder archetype, this was part of the shift in the higher esoteric beliefs of Western culture away from Christianity and towards science and technocracy, which eventually came to be closely tied up to the massive growth of the state via the modern bureaucratic apparatus. The Sage archetype of Western culture ceased to be the priest, bishop, and pope and became the technocrat, expert, and scientist.

But in relation to marriage, the loosening of the divorce laws had more to do with the other main change in the higher esoteric value structure that we can give the label *liberalism*. Liberalism's focus on individual freedom came to include the freedom to get divorced. More and more freedom was demanded until we eventually ended up with modern laws that allow divorce at any time and for any reason. The result has been that about half of all marriages now end in divorce. All of this is predicated on a move away from marriage as a duty wrapped up in Christian metaphysics and towards an ideal of marriage as being justified by romantic love. If romantic love is the higher esoteric justification for the marriage in the first place, then the loss of romantic love can also be the justification for its end (notwithstanding that lust is often mistaken for love in such matters). This is part of liberalism's prioritisation of individual over collective concerns. Again, we see how seemingly philosophical and abstract arguments at the higher esoteric level of being have real-world ramifications.

Because the family is the institution built around the Child-Parent pairing, what divorce means from an archetypal point of view is that the pairing gets broken at the socio-familial level. As a result, all members of the pair must go through another metamorphosis to establish a new equilibrium. How that resonates with each member depends on what archetypal stage they are going through. The Child archetype resonates primarily at the biological level of being, and so it is not a surprise to find that research shows that a common response by the Child to the divorce of the Parents is to regress to earlier developmental stages. This is evidence that the archetypal phase is being *restarted*, so to speak. Of course, the Mother and Father must also negotiate the reconfiguration of their own identities primarily at the socio-cultural and higher esoteric levels of being. The point, which is rather obvious in the case of the Child-Parent relationship, is that all members of an archetypal pairing are affected when the socio-cultural institution set up to maintain that pairing breaks down.

The second point is that broader social trends, including big changes in the belief structures of the higher esoteric, have a direct impact on the way in which the archetypes and archetypal pairs play out. Once upon a time, the Child-Parent pairing was as good as unbreakable in Western culture. Now, it is a very common occurrence that it get broken and that all members of the pair must deal with a reconfiguration of their identity.

The influence of larger social forces on the archetypal patterns will become much clearer as we now turn to the Orphan-Elder pairing, which has undergone far more substantial change in recent times in our culture. This change is related to the issues faced by the family. The move away from the extended family and towards the nuclear, which has accelerated in the post-war years in the West, emphasises the Child-Parent relationship at the expense of the Orphan-Elder (Child-Grandparent) within the familial domain.

As we are about to find out, that mirrors a trend in larger society away from the Orphan-Elder pairing and towards something very different. Let us now turn to the second archetypal pair.

The Orphan-Elder Pair

There are a number of reasons why the Orphan-Elder pairing is not well recognised in modern Western society, and so this section will necessarily include some discussion of the broader developments in our culture that we have already touched on in our discussion of the Elder archetype. There was one dimension of the Elder that we didn't go into much detail about earlier, and that is the socio-cultural role of the archetype in initiating the Orphans of society. The Orphan period of life is the beginning of the training and education that prepares us for our mature identities. Somebody needs to conduct that initiation and training, and that somebody is the Elder.

Now, it can be the case that the biological parent may actually fulfil the role of the Elder, especially in societies where the family is of great importance. However, even when this happens, we can still clearly distinguish between the two archetypal pairs. The Parent's primary job is the nurturance and care of the Child up until the point where the Child is ready to expand their identity beyond the family. The Elder's job is to assist the Orphan with the establishment of their wider identity in the economic, political, military, and religious realms.

For maximum clarity, let's give a formal definition of the Orphan-Elder relationship: the Orphan-Elder relationship exists when there is an Elder who is responsible for initiating the Orphan into an institution of society and who has a duty of care towards the initiate that includes a period of training and education that leads to full membership of the institution.

Note here that the word *institution* in modern English has come to imply a formal organisation such as a government department or corporation. Clearly, there are societies which have almost no such formal institutions. In such cases, we would be inclined to refer instead to *culture*. However, the Latin word *institutio* originally included to the set of meanings that we call *culture*, i.e., disposition, arrangement, law, or practice. To be clear, when we use *institution* in the discussion which follows, we are referring to both organisation and culture, which can be highly formal or highly informal depending on the situation and society in question.

Of course, when we frame it this way, we might argue that the family is also an institution and therefore that our definition entails the Child-Parent relationship. This is why we earlier differentiated between the familial realm and the socio-cultural. The Parents are most definitely in control of the familial realm, and there is no doubt that children are socialised in the family first before moving into wider society. But when a young person takes up membership in a socio-cultural institution, they are placed under the guidance of an Elder who represents that institution.

There are two main components to the Orphan-Elder relationship: initiation and training. These are two separate aspects of the same process, a process which is almost identical in form to the archetypal phases of life in that it can be broken up into a metamorphosis-stability pattern. Initiation is the metamorphosis. It signifies a change of state for the initiate. In most societies, initiation takes the form of rites and ceremonies that formally induct the initiate into the institution. It is the Elder archetype who inducts the Orphan. Depending on the nature of the initiation and the institution, the rites and ceremonies can be as short as a few hours, or they can last over an extended period of months or even years. A paradigm example can be found in the modern military. Boot camp is an extended initiation from which one graduates as a member of the military. The military is also useful as an example since it is one of the few institutions of modern society that has formal rites, including parades and ceremonies, as well as dress codes, fixed forms of address, and behaviour, etc. Many societies throughout history have followed this pattern of having highly formalised ceremonies of initiation, not just in the military domain but others too.

Once the initiation is over, the longer period of training begins. If the initiation is the metamorphosis, the training period maps to the stability part of the process, and it can last for many years. In ancient Sparta, a young man (Orphan) was paired with a mature warrior (Elder) at twelve years of age. It was the job of the Elder to induct the Orphan into the institutions of society while also providing military training. Since Sparta was famously a warrior-based society, this was a complete education for the young man, whose service continued until the age of thirty, at which point he was eligible to marry. In Australian Aboriginal society, a young man was taken away for initiation at puberty by the men of the tribe. The initiation itself was led by a tribal Elder and often lasted a number of months. After the formal initiation period, it was usually the maternal uncle who took on the role of Elder. Similar to the Spartan warrior, it was the uncle who had a duty of care to ensure the young man found his way in society. Most usually, the uncle was also responsible for finding his protégé a wife.

We can deduce from these brief examples an important difference between the Orphan-Elder pairing and the Child-Parent one. We only ever have one set of parents, but we may have many different kinds of Orphan-Elder relationships. Since almost every institution of society has a hierarchical structure, there is also a hierarchy of Elders. Initiation will usually be conducted by the higher-ranking Elders, while the training period is the responsibility of a lower-ranking one. For example, the military has its officer class, who are Elders of one kind, while the drill sergeant is also an Elder who is ranked lower but who has more day-to-day responsibility for the training of cadets (Orphans). Our relationship with the higher-ranking Elders is almost certainly going to be far more formal in nature than the one we have with the Elder that we deal with on a daily basis. For the former group, we say that our relationship is exoteric, while we have an esoteric relationship with the latter.

Since the Orphan-Elder relationship is primarily socio-cultural in nature, it is more likely to be exoteric by default, but a lot depends on the size of the institution in question. The larger the institution, the more likely the relationship will be formal, although there can be exceptions to this rule. We have probably all had the experience of that one schoolteacher who went above and beyond the call of duty and showed some special interest in us or tried to nurture our talent in a particular area. Most teachers don't do that, and other Elders don't necessarily do it either. The prescribed roles of society set a minimum standard of care. That is what we mean by exoteric in this case. The relationship is mostly formal. To go above and beyond that takes the relationship into the esoteric domain.

It is in the esoteric Orphan-Elder pairings where it is common to use a parental metaphor to describe the relationship. Jung sometimes referred to Freud as his second father because of the closeness of their bond, which went beyond the professional. Nevertheless, within our framework, we must insist that the relationship was an Orphan-Elder pairing because Freud was a recognised leader in the nascent field of psychoanalysis, and he initiated Jung into the early institution of that discipline while also being his main teacher. Of course, at that time, psychoanalysis was nothing more than a small group of enthusiasts, but that is certainly why the relationship between the two men was esoteric in nature. To say it again, the larger the institution, the more impersonal the Orphan-Elder relationship becomes, and the more exoteric form dominates over esoteric substance. Smaller groupings are always more esoteric. The relationship between Jesus and his disciples is perhaps the paradigmatic form of an esoteric Orphan-Elder relationship. Any more than twelve Orphans and the Elder relationship become exoteric and generic in nature.

Just as the Orphan may have multiple Elder relationships within the same institution, they can have a different relationship across the various domains of identity. Thus, an Orphan may have a different Elder for the military, economic, political, religious, and familial aspects of their identity. This division of responsibility is more common in complex societies with a strong division of labour as opposed to smaller and more organic cultures where the boundaries between the identities are less distinct. In the case where there are numerous different Orphan-Elder relationships, it is likely that only one or two will be esoteric in nature while the others will be exoteric. This makes sense on purely practical grounds since an individual only has so much time and focus to give. A full-time soldier will almost certainly have a military Elder as their primary relationship, while any other Elder relationships they have are likely to be less intensive and therefore more exoteric in nature.

One final general point to make about the Orphan-Elder relationship is our distinction from chapter two about elite initiation and training. This differs from the regular forms by being more intensive and esoteric in nature. Again, an easy example for us to understand from the modern world is sports, where the coach maps to the Elder archetype. Students who show genuine talent and motivation are given a more rigorous and extensive kind of training than those who are just playing for fun. In the former cases, we expect the coach to really push the Orphan to see what they are capable of and to drive them towards the highest standard of performance. As a result, this kind of Orphan-Elder relationship is almost certainly going to be esoteric in nature since the training is of a small, elite group, rather than a broad mass. Each domain of identity has its own elite forms of initiation. Thus, we have special forces in the military, esoteric religious training, and special pathways into the highest echelons of politics.

To summarise the points just made, we say that the Orphan-Elder relationship exists when Elders initiate Orphans into the institutions of society and provide them with an extended period of training. The initiation usually entails formal ceremonies and rites that explicitly induct the initiate into the institution. Initiation is the metamorphosis that changes the status of the Orphan to initiate, student, protégé, or whatever other labels we may want to use. They are now formally members of the institution and they begin to pursue the long period of training and education that leads to full membership. Because institutions usually have hierarchies, there can be multiple Orphan-Elder relationships. The more abstract and formal ones we call exoteric, while the personal ones are usually esoteric in nature. Finally, we note that an individual can have multiple Orphan-Elder relationships across the different domains of identity. This is more likely in complex societies.

Putting all this together, it's not hard to see why the Orphan-Elder relationship is not well recognised in modern Western society. Firstly, we got rid of most of the formal rites of passage that signify the initiation of the relationship. Secondly, the complexity of modern society means we usually have multiple Elder relationships. Thirdly, the scale of modern society emphasises the exoteric over the esoteric, meaning that the relationships we do form are usually not intimate enough to generate an esoteric bond. Finally, the fast-paced nature of modern life means that Orphan-Elder relationships typically do not last very long.

Despite this lack of overt recognition in the general culture, the Orphan-Elder relationship is very common in modern works of literature and film, although it tends to show up mostly in genres which have a fantasy element, including science fiction. In the Jungian sense, we would say that the Orphan-Elder is present in the collective unconscious, but not in the collective consciousness.

Perhaps the best-known fictional example of the Orphan-Elder relationship in recent times comes from the initial *Star Wars* trilogy. Luke Skywalker is the archetypal Orphan who has not one but two Elders in Obi-Wan Kenobi and Yoda. There are also two shadow Elders in the form of Darth Vader and Palpatine, who are trying to lure Luke towards a very different kind of initiation (*the dark side*, the empire). Especially in relation to the scenes with Yoda, we see that Luke receives explicit education and training from the Elder. However, the Elder's role is not just about explicit instruction but also implicit. They lead by example. This is not just related to technical performance but more subtle aspects of the role such as behaviour, speech, style etc. An Elder embodies the style of the archetype they manifest, whether they be a Warrior, Ruler, or Sage. In doing so, they provide a standard that the Orphan can aspire to.

Another prime example of the Orphan-Elder relationship from modern film can be seen in the movie *The Matrix*, especially the extended training scenes where we see Morpheus give personal instruction to Neo. Note that in the case of both Luke Skywalker and Neo, what they are being inducted into is an institution of which the Elder is the recognised leader. The Elder is embodying an archetype, but that archetype is consonant with the goals of the institution. The Orphan must learn what those goals are and begin to contribute towards them. That is also part of their education and training. The Orphan's induction into an economic, political, or military establishment is about agreeing to support the mission of that establishment.

Thus, Luke Skywalker joins the rebel fighters and contributes to the battle against the empire. Neo joins the crew of the Nebuchadnezzar and takes part in their battle against the agents of the matrix. To take just two other famous modern stories that feature the Orphan-Elder relationship, Harry Potter is joining the institution of Hogwarts under the leadership of Dumbledore, while Frodo Baggins joins the fellowship of the ring under the guidance of Gandalf. All of these fictional stories include the general properties of the Orphan-Elder relationship that we have outlined in this section. What the popularity of these stories shows is that we in the modern West still have an appetite for and an unconscious understanding of the Orphan-Elder pairing. Let's now drill down deeper into this relationship.

The Dynamics of the Orphan-Elder Transition

Now that we have established the basis of the Orphan-Elder relationship, we can turn to the question of the dynamics of the metamorphosis that must occur to create it. We have already prefigured the core issue with that dynamic with our discussion of the Orphan archetype from chapter two where we said that the Orphan must make a break with the parents in order to forge their own identity. Formulated in terms of the archetypal pairs, we say that the Child-Parent relationship must give way to the Orphan-Elder. That is what is required for the Orphan to establish its identity outside the familial sphere. Unlike the Child-Parent metamorphosis, where it is only the Parents who must relinquish a past archetypal identity, for the Orphan-Elder metamorphosis we have two transitions required: the Child must become an Orphan and the Parent must become an Elder. That's how it looks at first glance, although, as we will see shortly, there is a third crucial transition as well.

The Child must make the leap into the Orphan archetype, and the Parent must make the leap into something else. What is that something else? Of course, a Parent always remains a parent in the biological sense, and the family usually remains a family, barring a dramatic, although fairly common, occurrence where something happens to break it up. Our focus on the nuclear family, which is a relatively recent development in the West, obscures a general tendency which seems to operate across cultures. What we find in the anthropological literature is that many societies will explicitly deprecate the status of the parent by way of taboos or changed standards of behaviour once the Child has come of age. Freud analysed such taboos as protective measures designed to mitigate the risk of incest with the onset of sexual maturity. Perhaps there is some truth to that. However, what our archetypal model suggests is that the deprecation of the Child-Parent relationship is done to allow the Orphan-Elder to become dominant. Even in the safety-obsessed modern age, the overprotective Parent is often seen as a risk to the Child's development.

One way to represent the metamorphosis that the Parent must go through is to say that they themselves must become an Elder. By our earlier definition, this is not strictly true, but it works in a more abstract sense. The Elder is about guidance and oversight. That seems to be a fitting description of the role that Parents must step into by allowing their children to become Orphans. They are no longer called on to directly determine the Child's actions but to watch over them from a distance. Most Parents will naturally transition into something like this role anyway, but it can happen that the Parent does not want to let go. This leads to a pathological state that is relatively common in the modern West with our emphasis on the nuclear family. Since Mothers are usually the primary carers of the Child, it should be no surprise to find that they are the Parent who most struggles to let go. This pattern is common enough that Jung gave it its own archetype: the Devouring Mother. The Devouring Mother strives to keep her Child dependent well beyond the time when it is appropriate and healthy. In extreme cases, she may psychologically and even physically abuse the Child to maintain this dependence. This is known as *Munchausen by Proxy*. To be clear, the Devouring Mother phenomenon is almost never a conscious choice. The Mother is not deliberately and consciously setting out to keep her Child dependent; it happens unconsciously.

The temptation towards over-protection can be exacerbated if the Child is struggling with its own transition into the Orphan archetype. As Jung pointed out, because of the psychic difficulty of the Orphan transition, it is a very common scenario that individuals will revert back to childish behaviours. In that case, it may not be enough for the Parents to step back and allow the

Child space; they may need to explicitly encourage the Orphan metamorphosis. How many of us were told by our parents something along the lines of, "Act your age, mister. You're not a kid anymore!" when we behaved like a Child beyond the time where it was appropriate. This kind of *tough love* has fallen out of favour in recent decades, which is part of the reason why the Devouring Mother pattern has become far more prevalent.

All of this reiterates the main point we are making with the concept of the archetypal pairs, which is that the difficulties of the metamorphosis are not just related to the individual and their own struggles but to the requirement that the archetypal pair play their part too. When this doesn't happen, things can go awry for both members of the pair. It may be that the Child does not want to become an Orphan. It may be that the Parent does not want the Child to become an Orphan. Both of these tendencies are usually present to some degree and need to be overcome. It takes effort from both members of the archetypal pair to overcome their specific challenges so that they may play the role that the other requires of them. In this case, what is required is that both members of the Child-Parent pairing must relinquish their old identities. The Parent has to give up the primacy of their role in the Child's life and allow them to become an Orphan. The Child must give up the security of the Parent relationship and step into the wider world.

This gives us two possible pathologies. We have already talked about the first, which is the Parent who will not let go, aka the Devouring Mother. The second is the Child who will not take the step into the Orphan phase. This is sometimes called the Peter Pan Complex after the fictional story about the boy who never grows up. Both of these pathologies are related to the unwillingness of either partner to relinquish the Child-Parent pairing. However, there is another pathology which is related to the other side of the equation. The Child-Parent pairing must give way to the Orphan-Elder relationship. That can only happen if there is an Elder there who is able to form that relationship with the Orphan. What happens when the Elder is not there?

There are two primary pathologies that can occur with the formation of the Orphan-Elder pair. The first is when the exoteric roles disappear i.e., the social basis for the Orphan-Elder pairing disappears. The second pathology is when those exoteric roles no longer fulfil the higher esoteric needs of the individuals. We will examine this second pathology later in the book when we analyse the life of a man who felt the absence of esoteric initiation as an existential crisis: Martin Luther. We will spend the rest of this chapter looking at the first pathology, which is when either the Elder or the Orphan role goes missing.

To understand what it means for the Elder archetype to go missing, we need to remember a point we made earlier about how there can be multiple different Elders for each domain of identity: the familial, economic, political, military, and religious. The absence of an Elder in one or two of these domains may not cause much of a problem as long as the Orphan can find an Elder in another domain. For example, in Shakespeare's great play, when Hamlet tells Ophelia to get herself to a nunnery, what he is saying is that she should escape the toxic court environment and take up the life of a religious anchorite. This exchange of a political for a religious identity entails a new Orphan-Elder relationship and a new initiation. It is the substitution of one path for another.

This option may be theoretically available to most Orphans who find their chosen life path blocked. However, it can happen that more extreme cases arise whereby all opportunity for initiation goes away. In such cases, no Orphan-Elder relationship can form. Fortunately for us, there is a prime example of just that dynamic from recent Western history and it offers a way for us to investigate what happens when the Orphan-Elder relationship cannot form.

A Case Study on Feminism

We must remember here that the metamorphosis-stability pattern holds in relation to the Orphan-Elder pair, just as it does for the individual archetypes. In the socio-cultural domain, the metamorphosis usually takes the form of formal rites of passage that signify to both the individual and society that the Orphan is now a member of an institution and is going to undertake a period of training to become a full member. Since the formal rites which constitute the initiation period are always carried out by an Elder, the metamorphosis in the socio-cultural domain entails the formation of the Orphan-Elder relationship. In the biological-familial domain, however, things are a little less straightforward, but there is also a metamorphosis period and also the formation of an Orphan-Elder relationship. At least, that's the way it's traditionally been for women.

We have already noted a common sexual asymmetry throughout history and across cultures where women are mostly denied entry to the socio-cultural institutions of society. In such circumstances, women still receive initiation into the religious institutions society, but their main initiation has typically been marriage. For men, we would want to call marriage the onset of the Adult period of life, because men have traditionally gone through the formation of their socio-cultural identity before getting married. In other words, they have completed the Orphan archetype. In such traditional circumstances, the groom is always quite a lot older than the bride for this reason.

By contrast, the traditional age of marriage for women has been shortly after puberty. That's one reason we would want to classify marriage as the rite of passage that marks the onset of the Orphan phase of life for women. What women are being initiated into in this case is the family of their husband, and that is where they expect to find both their Orphan and their Adult identity. Other evidence for this reading of marriage as an Orphan initiation ceremony is the fact that the bride (not the groom) is given away by her parents, which is indicative of the deprecation of the Child-Parent relationship.

The question in relation to the Orphan-Elder pair, then, is if marriage is the rite of passage initiating the Orphan phase of life for women in traditional circumstances, who becomes their Elder during the training and education phase that follows? The answer, of course, is one or both of her mother-in-law or grandmother-in-law. Extended families are the most common living arrangement across cultures, so there is a very good chance that these Elders will be living in the same house as the bride. But, even if that's not the case, they would be expected in most cultures to take an active role in the new household, providing guidance and perhaps even training to the new arrival. Thus, marriage is the Orphan rite of passage for young women, which leads into a metamorphosis period where the young wife comes under the guidance of a matriarch of some kind, who will help her come to grips with her new identity in the household of her husband. In short, we see that, in this traditional setup, women form the Orphan-Elder pairing in the familial domain just as men do in the socio-cultural.

The reason all this is relevant is because the case study we are about to undertake revolves around marriage rites and practices in Western society and how a major change in these affected the Orphan metamorphosis for a certain demographic of young women. As it turns out, Western society has had an unusual variation on the traditional marriage pattern since medieval times. The set of practices followed has been given the name of the Western European Marriage Pattern (WEMP). With the increasing dominance of the western and northern European cultures from the time of the Reformation onwards, this pattern has become common in the whole of the West and is now taken for granted, so that we don't realise how important it was in the rise of modern feminism.

The core features of the WEMP included an older average age of marriage among the general population relative to most cultures. This was especially unusual among women, who often married in their twenties or even early thirties. Another feature was the relative prevalence of the nuclear family as opposed to the extended family. There were rather high rates of celibacy among the general population, and, finally, there was relative freedom in choosing a marriage partner as opposed to the arranged marriages that occur in many cultures.

Of crucial importance to the history we are about to unfold is the fact that the WEMP did not apply to aristocratic families. These followed the more cross-culturally common practice whereby women were married shortly after puberty, while their male counterparts began a period of education and training to prepare them for roles at the top of the institutions of society. We see a prime example of this dynamic in Shakespeare's *Romeo and Juliet.* Juliet is not even fourteen years old when Paris comes courting. The young woman is not enthusiastic, but her mother tries to encourage her by noting that some of her friends have already been married. The implication is that marriage at thirteen was not uncommon for a woman of Juliet's pedigree at the beginning of the 17th century. (In most European nations, women were legally able to marry at twelve years of age all the way until the mid-19th century).

Where the WEMP was anthropologically unusual was among the general population. Because western Europe was relatively poor, most families could not afford the dowry which would help a newly married couple to establish themselves. As a result, it was common for both men and women to spend years working before marriage in order to save money. This meant that working-class women received a similar Orphan initiation to men via paid employment, although they were mostly engaged as maids in the households of the wealthy. The upshot of all this is that aristocratic women in Europe were the odd ones out by getting married in their early to mid-teens. The average age of marriage for the rest of the population was late teens to early twenties for women and late twenties for men. This state of affairs continued all the way into the 19th century, when social trends began to change.

The WEMP implied that aristocratic brides were much younger than their husbands. Women could be married in their early teens, while men were expected to establish themselves in society first. One of the reasons this became problematic in the 19th century was because it became desirable to marry someone your own age. This was closely related to the idea of marrying for love, which started to become an ideal that the upper classes aimed for, whereas marriage had previously been almost entirely about economic and political calculations. The result was that aristocratic women no longer wanted to marry older men. Can it be a coincidence that this is basically the plot of *Romeo and Juliet* (Juliet doesn't want to marry Paris) and that the works of Shakespeare more generally enjoyed a surge in popularity in the 19th century?

Let's think through the logistics of this. In Shakespeare's time, Juliet was expected to get married at thirteen years of age. She would have moved in with Paris and had children almost immediately. Her life would have revolved around the domestic sphere with a specific focus on raising her own children and taking care of the household. That was the normal life course for an aristocratic woman. By the 19th century, even if Romeo wasn't in the picture, Juliet would have denied Paris' marriage request on the grounds that he was too old for her, and her parents would likely have agreed. However, aristocratic men were still expected to establish themselves before marriage. There were no eligible bachelors of thirteen years of age for Juliet to marry, and in any case legislative changes meant that such a marriage was no longer legal. Putting all this together, the only course of action for Juliet was to wait until she was the same age as the average suitor, i.e., late teens. And herein lay the entire problem, because there was nothing else for Juliet to do during her teenage years.

We have to remember that in the 19th century there were no education or work opportunities for aristocratic women. While it was common for such women to receive some education, this was done in the family home itself, not in school, and certainly not in university. Thus, the new practice of the bride waiting to be the same age as the groom had condemned aristocratic women to a long period of idleness and boredom. They were stuck in the family home during their teenage years with no real opportunity to do anything outside it. This was in contrast to working-class women, who were still going off to work to save money for their marriage.

In our archetypal terms, what had happened was that the metamorphosis (marriage) that marks the beginning of the Orphan phase of life had been delayed for aristocratic women only, while it remained unchanged for aristocratic men and the general population. In terms of our archetypal pairs, the Orphan-Elder relationship could not form. Using our archetypal transition diagram, it looks as follows:-

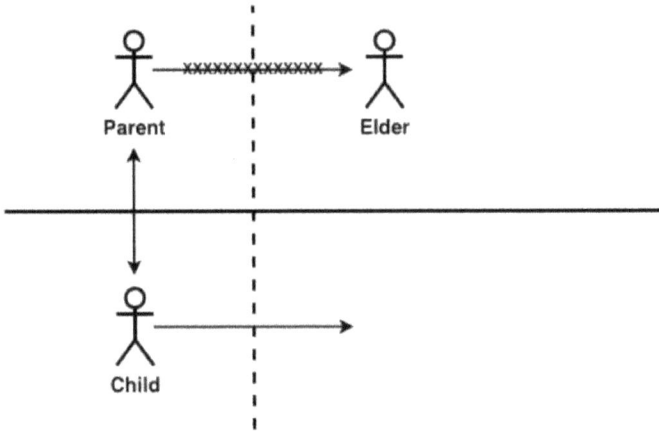

Here is where the logic of our archetypal pair concept really comes into its own. If there is no Orphan-Elder relationship to step into, our model predicts that young women would get stuck in the Child-Parent pairing. This is exactly what happened, quite literally so, because the women were stuck in the homes of their parents at the age where they were supposed to forge their own identity outside of the family.

In relation to the archetypal metamorphosis, we must remember our differentiation between the biological, socio-cultural, and higher esoteric levels of being. The biological carries on irrespective. Aristocratic women were still reaching puberty at the same time as always. They had become sexually mature but had no outlet for their sexuality. Doesn't it seem incredibly coincidental that the Victorian era suddenly developed very strict societal norms around sex? Doesn't it also seem coincidental that Freud would later diagnose many of the psychological problems he saw as stemming from an unfulfilled sex drive?

But the problems were not just related to biology or psychology. Aristocratic women were left in limbo in the socio-cultural sphere too. Apart from marriage, there was still no recognised Adult identity for young Orphan women to work towards. The economic, political, and military pathways available to their aristocratic male counterparts were closed to them as they always had been. The final nail in the coffin was the loss of belief in the Christian faith that took hold, especially among the aristocracy, in the 19th century. Hamlet could tell Ophelia to get herself to a nunnery, and in Shakespeare's time that might have been a possibility. But nobody would have understood it in the 19th century. Like the rest of the aristocracy, young women went through the motions of religious observance, but they felt no esoteric connection to the church or the faith. Putting it all together, we can see that there were no available Orphan-Elder relationships for aristocratic Orphan women in any of the domains of identity. The familial, economic, political, military, and religious Orphan transitions were all blocked.

Given all this, it's no surprise that the 19th century was full of literature featuring young women stuck in unfulfilling domestic situations. The beautiful young girl trapped at home in the house of her parents shows up in Emily Bronte, Jane Austen, Henrik Ibsen, and many Russian writers. The literary trope of the aristocratic woman fainting on the couch and then taking to her bed became so common that it got its own name: *brain fever*. A hapless doctor was brought in to make a diagnosis, but there was nothing physically wrong. The real problem was psychosomatic in nature.

And this leads us directly to another major development that arose out of the same archetypal dynamic: the arrival of psychoanalysis. It is no coincidence that both Freud and Jung were educated in medicine. What they came to realise was that their patients didn't have anything physically wrong with them. That led to the search for psychological explanations. What demographic constituted Freud and Jung's primary patient base? Of course, it was none other than young aristocratic women.

Take Freud's most famous study, usually called the *Dora Case*. Dora's real name was Ida Bauer. She was eighteen years of age when her father referred her. Ida Bauer was exactly the kind of young woman we have just described. She was of the aristocracy (her brother would later become the Austrian foreign minister). She was stuck at home with her parents with no independent identity of her own. She fell into the kinds of neuroses that filled the pages of 19th-century fiction and then became the main object of study for Freud and Jung. Some have attributed Freud's fixation on sex to his own personal fetishes. Actually, he was certainly right that sexual frustration played a big role in the problems that his young female patients had. No surprise, then, that the incident which made Ida Bauer's father send her to Freud involved a sexual advance made on her by an older man. It didn't help matters that Ida knew that her father was cheating on her mother, although having a mistress was not unusual for a wealthy man of that era.

Within our archetypal model, the problem faced by young women like Ida Bauer is very clear. Puberty is the natural time for the beginning of our Orphan phase of life for both biological and psychological reasons. But what Victorian society had done was to delay the primary socio-cultural metamorphosis (marriage) for young aristocratic women. We should remember again here that the Orphan-Elder relationship is primarily socio-cultural in nature; it is about being inducted into an institution of society (including the family). To not be inducted is the equivalent of having no social identity at all. Even the loveless marriages of earlier times provided young women with structure, jobs to be done, children to raise, and a social network to cultivate. The alternative was nothing. Rather than extroverting themselves into new social roles, aristocratic Orphan women were forced back into introversion, where they developed the kinds of psychological problems that Freud and Jung would diagnose.

What makes the case of aristocratic women in the 19th century so poignant from an archetypal point of view is that a very specific demographic suffered the disappearance of the Orphan-Elder metamorphosis across all the available domains of identity, even the old religious fallback of the Christian priest no longer worked. We can represent the problem on our identity diagram from chapter two as follows:-

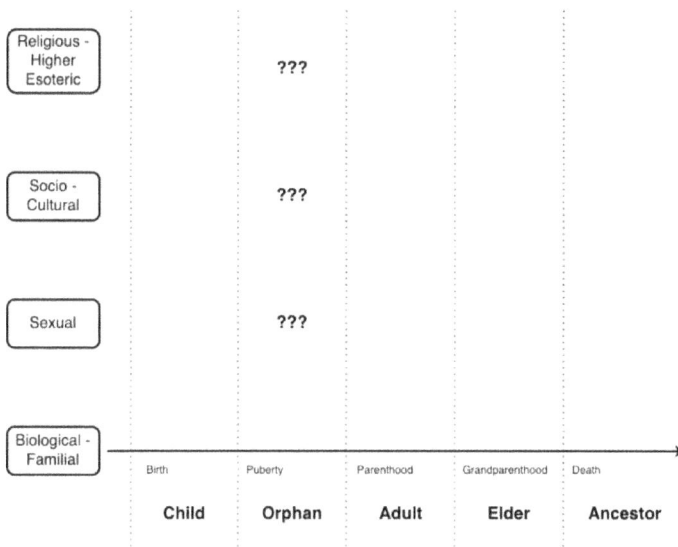

Religious - Higher Esoteric		???				
Socio - Cultural		???				
Sexual		???				
Biological - Familial						
	Birth	Puberty	Parenthood	Grandparenthood	Death	
	Child	**Orphan**	**Adult**	**Elder**	**Ancestor**	

But what really makes the plight of women in the 19th century so valuable to archetypology is that we know what happened in the aftermath. Aristocratic women had no available Orphan-Elder relationship. This created a crisis of identity. Just as our physical body responds to a pathology by initiating the healing process, we can see that the archetypal pathology that beset aristocratic women triggered a response on several fronts.

The first response is the one we have already touched on: the arrival of psychoanalysis. We have noted several times in the book that the loss of the Christian faith was tied in with a new version of the higher esoteric that included both liberalism and scientific materialism. It was this latter development that was related to psychoanalysis. Jung and Freud were exponents of science and garnered much of their reputation from being seen as such. This places them in the role of religious Elders since they represented the higher esoteric belief structure that was becoming dominant.

What is particularly interesting in this respect is how similar psychoanalysis was to the old practice of confession within the Catholic church. Whereas their parents only wanted to tell young women what to do and how to behave, Freud and Jung offered a listening ear, just as the Catholic priest used to. The two men took the concerns of their young female patients seriously and attempted to alleviate their problems. Freud and Jung had stepped into the Sage archetype. They offered their patients a sophisticated esoteric practice that was, especially in Jung's case, very similar to religious observance in that it invited the patient to reflect on some of the deeper questions of life and psyche. Therefore, we can say that Freud and Jung had re-created the Orphan-Elder pairing at the religious-higher esoteric domain of identity. Let's add that to our identity diagram:-

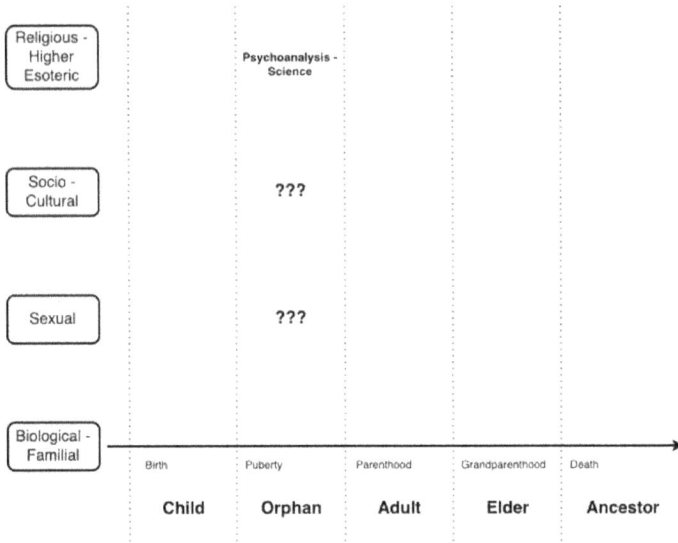

Both psychoanalysis and the expression of the problems faced by aristocratic women in 19ᵗʰ century literature belong to what we have generally called the esoteric aspect of existence. These expressed both the psychological and existential sides of the conundrum that young women had found themselves in. But it was the next item down from the higher esoteric in our identity diagram that has arguably had the greatest impact.

Remembering yet again the point we have touched on several times now that the normal pattern cross culturally is for young women to be married shortly after puberty and to receive their primary initiation into the households of their husbands, and remembering also that aristocratic women in Europe had been unusual in following this pattern rather than the WEMP, what occurred when that familial option was no longer available was the demand that the socio-cultural domain be opened up to women. This was the social and political movement that we all know as *feminism*.

From our archetypal point of view, what feminism did was very clear. It created pathways to the socio-cultural identities that had previously been denied to women. Women were brought into the workforce (economic identity) while also being given equal political rights (political identity). Later, they were even able to join the military. Alongside access to formal education, including university, young women were now able to begin the development of their socio-cultural identity in the same way and at the same time of life as their male counterparts. Aristocratic women ended up joining the other demographics of Western culture (aristocratic men and the general public) in following the WEMP both in terms of age of marriage and also by the desire to pursue a socio-cultural identity prior to marriage. We can see that this development was closely linked to the third item in our identity list with the increasing liberalisation of sexual norms allowing all members of society to develop a sexual identity prior to marriage as well. We can now add these to our identity diagram as follows:-

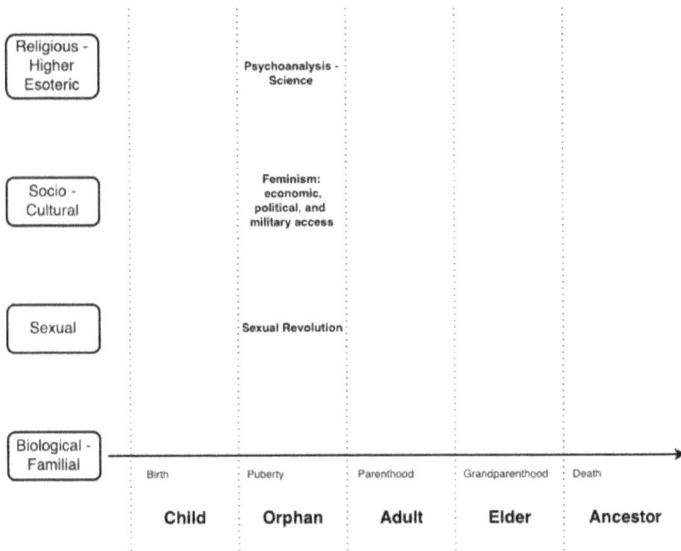

All of this lends great weight to our archetypal analysis since we see that three seemingly unrelated societal movements (psychoanalysis, feminism, the sexual revolution) can all be diagnosed as stemming from the same underlying archetypal dynamic. Aristocratic women had been thrown into a kind of limbo where their teenage years, normally a time of great growth, had been rendered meaningless and void. Because the Orphan-Elder pairing had been made unavailable, they were stuck in the Child-Parent one. What both psychoanalysis and feminism offered was the re-establishment of the Orphan-Elder relationship. It was, of course, a very different set of Elders from the ones that were available beforehand, but it offered all of the main qualities that Orphans require from their Elders: guidance, education, training, and initiation into the institutions of society. Freud and Jung filled not just a practical role that was similar to that of the Catholic confessional; they were also representatives of "science" and therefore of the new set of values that had taken over in the higher esoteric conceptions of Western culture. They played the role of Sage archetype, offering initiation into a new religious identity. In the socio-cultural sphere, women now had access to the same set of Elders as men, whether that be in school and university, in the democratic political process, or in the workforce.

In summary, what we have seen in this case study is a complete transformation in the set of identities available to aristocratic women as a demographic. Gone was the old Orphan initiation of marriage. This was moved into the Adult phase of life alongside their male counterparts and the general public. Women would no longer receive education and training in the household but in the socio-cultural institutions of society. It is curious in this respect that these changes coincided with the move away from extended families and into the modern nuclear family pattern. In that new pattern, the old female Elder role of mother-in-law or grandmother-in-law became redundant, and it is here that the cultural changes that were specific to aristocratic women joined a more general change that was taking place in Western society, one that was affecting everybody. The story we have just told implied that aristocratic women had re-established the Orphan-Elder relationship that had gone missing. But that is only partly true. To understand the ambiguity here, we now need to revisit a topic we touched on earlier in the book and look at the loss of the Elder archetype in the 20th century.

The Loss of the Elder

In chapter two, we analysed the problematic nature of the Elder archetype in the modern West in relation to the major shift in our metaphysical and theological understanding of the world that began in the 19th century. In that discussion, we took a more existential approach to the Elder archetype, which fits with the confrontation with death that the Elder must go through on their personal journey. In this chapter, we have been more concerned with an anthropological view of the Elder, especially in their relationship with the Orphan. Our goal has been to identify how the Elder archetype functions in a social sense. We noted two of the main functions as initiation and training. In addition, we have seen that the Elder may also provide guidance and counselling to their protégés. These are the traditional functions of the Elder, but these were largely lost in the 20th century in Western society as a result of a change in the higher esoteric beliefs of our culture.

We can contrast modern Western society with cultures that are perhaps on the other end of the spectrum in relation to reverence for the Elders. The anthropological literature tells us that Elders had the primary leadership role in hunter-gatherer tribes. This reverence for age was certainly related to the higher esoteric beliefs of such cultures in that the Elders were seen to be closest to the gods and this made them sacred. But it's also probable that there were practical reasons why Elders would dominate in such societies. Elders had the accumulated knowledge of a lifetime of experience behind them. In a world without written records, the value of that knowledge must have been great. Furthermore, the small-scale groupings of family and tribe made the dissemination of that knowledge through direct personal relationships practical. We can speculate that Elders may thrive whenever decentralised and small-scale groupings of people exist. That is not the case in our time.

Complex modern societies rely on large, hierarchical institutions governed by formal rules and laws. We know from our earlier discussion that this implies a far more exoteric set of relationships than the esoteric ones which dominate in small-scale groups. Bureaucracies take this exoteric quality to an extreme. A bureaucracy is, in large part, a machine whose parts turn according to the rules imposed from above. In large bureaucracies, age and experience do not automatically confer any special prestige or position. The leadership roles that in many cultures automatically fall to the most senior people are now determined by formal rules of promotion. What's more, because of the hierarchical nature of such organisations, only a small number of people can ascend to leadership positions. Power and authority accrue to the top of the pyramid, leaving little opportunity for informal (esoteric) influence at the lower levels.

If we recall the primary functions of the Elder as initiation, education, training, guidance, and leadership, we can see that the modern bureaucracy undermines the leadership function by rewarding not those who are the most experienced but those who are most able to follow the latest ideological fashions. In fact, the cutthroat nature of corporate politics promotes a kind of ideological arms race as competition over the limited number of positions at the top of the hierarchy increases. The question of the truth of such ideologies becomes secondary to their primary function of sorting out internal organisational politics. What is important is that the ideologies are constantly changing so that would-be challengers for the limited number of roles at the top of the tree are always scrambling to keep up. None of this is consonant with the Elder's focus on wisdom.

Meanwhile, the Elder's other main functions have been usurped by the arrival of the "experts". The initiation of new employees and the training of the general workforce have become the responsibilities of universities and HR departments which do not conduct these practices according to any tradition that has been handed down from one generation to another but according to whatever latest theory is fashionable. Even guidance and counselling is now organised through professional roles such as psychologists rather than informally organised mentor relationships. In short, bureaucracies are full of experts, and the experts have pushed out Elders. To the extent that bureaucracies have taken over the economic sphere of the modern West, they have removed the Elder archetype from that sphere.

What about the other domains of identity? In relation to modern politics, there are no Elders, since political participation in the democratic process does not require initiation, training, or guidance. Most people do not join a political party but rather vote for whoever they want at the time based on whatever criteria is important to them. Whatever we think about that, there is no space for Elders in such a system.

The military might seem like a domain that still has the Elder role since it has formal rites and ceremonies and fixed forms of address and behaviour. That is true to some extent, however the military has also become little more than a giant bureaucracy which is the domain of experts, not Elders. Furthermore, the majority of the population no longer undergoes military training in most Western nations.

Finally, we have the higher esoteric domain of science, which we now know is a main component of the religious identity of the modern West. Just like democratic politics, modern science makes the Elder role redundant, not just because most of the public is not actively involved in it, but because the underlying philosophy is that any position can be disproven by new data. Respect for authority and tradition plays no role.

The last sphere where the average person had a chance at being an Elder was the family, where the Grandparent role maps to the Elder phase of life. But the trend away from multi-generational living has removed even that option. The dominance of the nuclear family pattern has translated into the cultural dominance of the Parent archetype at the expense of the Grandparent. Parents now expect to have complete freedom to raise their children as they see fit. The input of Grandparents is no longer welcomed or even tolerated in the way it once was. What's more, parental norms are also no longer set by tradition but in reference to the latest theories. The technocracy has extended its reach inside the nuclear family via the medical, psychiatric, and educational systems, all of which interface primarily with the Parents. The wisdom of the Elder has been once again disintermediated by the ideology of the experts.

The point here is not to draw any moral judgements about any of this. Rather, we are simply laying out the case for why and how the Elder role has disappeared from society. From an anthropological point of view, the functions of the Elder have now almost entirely been handed over to the experts, and this makes sense when we understand that technocracy and science took over as the dominant guardians of the higher esoteric of the West beginning in the late 19th century but accelerating strongly in the post-war years of the 20th. When we analyse these developments from our archetypal model, we can see that the situation for Elders in the 20th and 21st centuries is almost identical to that of aristocratic women in the 19th. The archetypal role has simply gone away. It's not hard to see why. The advent of capitalism, science, and technocracy has resulted in rapid technological and cultural change. This significantly reduces the relevance of the practical skills and experience collected throughout a lifetime. Reverence for age, the underlying principle of the Elder, makes little practical sense in such a social milieu.

Thinking about this dynamic in terms of the archetypal pairs, we can now diagram the Orphan-Elder relationship from the other direction. It's not a question of Elders being missing in relation to would-be Orphans but of Orphans not being available to would-be Elders. Just like the other archetypes, Elders must have their own metamorphosis. The transition in this case is from Adult to Elder, but that transition requires the formation of the Orphan-Elder pair. If there are no Orphans available, the pair does not get formed, and the Adult to Elder transition cannot happen. This is how it looks on our diagram:-

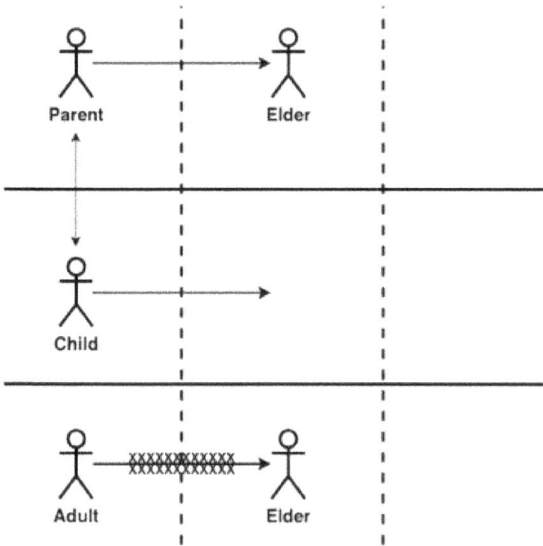

With no available Orphans with which to form the Orphan-Elder relationship, our model yet again makes a firm prediction about what should happen, namely, that the individual gets stuck in the Adult archetype. This is exactly what seems to have been borne out in the 20th century. Once upon a time, the Elder role began in midlife. It has now become synonymous with retirement, the end of one's Adult economic identity. Gone is the expectation that the Elder needs to transmit their knowledge to the next generation by initiating them and then providing an extended period of education and training. Even retirement has lost most of its Elder connotations. If anything, it is now seen as a second adolescence, a chance to once again become carefree and fun-loving. What has gone missing are the Elder functions of leadership, initiation, education, guidance, and counselling.

It's tempting to say that all of this is the result of the rapid pace of societal and technological change. But it's also the case that the above dynamic is the natural outcome of the doctrine of liberalism, which we identified as being one of the major changes that took place in the higher esoteric belief structure of the West in the 20th century. The freedom to choose one's own identity requires there to be no Elder archetypes since the Elder's role is to offer, initiate, and guide the Orphan through an identity formation process. Implied in this is that the Orphan accepts the role that has been offered to them rather than creates one of their own. Thus, the breakdown of the Orphan-Elder relationship is a feature, not a bug, when viewed from the doctrine of liberalism.

All of this raises a question. If the Orphan-Elder pairing has gone missing, doesn't this contradict the conclusion we drew at the end of the last section? After all, didn't aristocratic women solve the problem of their own missing Orphan-Elder relationship through psychoanalysis and access to the socio-cultural institutions of society? Furthermore, are we justified in saying that experts are not Elders? After all, our technical definition of Elder is someone who initiates and trains Orphans in the institutions of society. If experts carry out that task, then they are Elders by definition.

Let's weigh this issue up from both perspectives.

Taking stock of the changes that began happening in the 19th century and especially the second half of that century, we see several major themes that emerged as dominant value sets in the higher esoteric domain of Western culture. We have already identified science and liberalism as two of those, and we can add democracy and technocracy as the primary developments in the political sphere. Related to all these was the rollout of mass education, which we must understand was tightly coupled with the desire on the part of the state to disintermediate the church. The belief structure promulgated by the new education system had all the elements we have outlined: science, technocracy, capitalism, and liberalism.

When viewed this way, it does seem like this new pattern fits our description of the Orphan-Elder relationship. School teachers and university lecturers take over from priests and bishops as the primary Elders who are initiating the Orphans into the new belief structure. The experts and technocrats take their place as Elders in the economic and political spheres. Since the schools and universities had become the training grounds for the technocracy, we see an initiatory pipeline that channels Orphans into the institutions of society. It is true that age and seniority are not the determinants of who is and is not an Elder in such a system, but there was nothing about age and seniority in our definition of the Orphan–Elder relationship. We simply said that the Elder is the person who inducts the Orphan into the institutions of society. Therefore, the new system still fits our definition, and we have to say that the teachers, professors, experts, and technocrats are all Elders serving the higher esoteric ideals of science, technocracy, capitalism, and liberalism.

What makes the new system hard to come to grips with is that it differs from the old one in that the formal ceremonies and rites of passage that mark the Orphan–Elder relationship were largely abandoned. Remember our earlier definition of religion as the exoteric institutions and practices that represent the higher esoteric beliefs. In the case of the Catholic Church, the exoteric nature of the religion is very pronounced with intricate organisational dynamics, formal roles and modes of address, formal ceremonies and rites, clothing, buildings, paintings, sculptures, and other ornamental features. The technocracy definitely has an exoteric aspect to it, but it is far less overt than a traditional religion. Part of the reason for that is that the technocracy sees itself in opposition to traditional religion, and one of the ways it represents that opposition is precisely not to have overt and intricate exoteric structures. But the fact that the technocracy has eschewed formal practices does not make it any less of a body of thought and values that are amenable to initiation. To use more common modern words, we would say that the initiation into the technocracy is more about culture or ideology than exoteric membership. To use the dichotomy we have returned to many times in this book, we would say that the technocracy is esoteric in nature while the Christian church is exoteric and formal in nature.

To draw out this point, let's return to the example of psychoanalysis. We have already demonstrated that Freud and Jung had taken on a role very similar to that of a Christian priest by becoming esoteric Elders (Sage archetypes) to the Orphans of the early 20th century. Since psychoanalysis was a scientific discipline, its ascendancy at the expense of the church was consonant with the shift from Christian theology to scientific metaphysics that was taking place in the general culture. However, when we look at the specifics of the Orphan-Elder relationship created by psychoanalysis, we notice a crucial difference. The Christian priest offers an esoteric relationship of counselling where that is desired, but they also offer exoteric membership in the church with all the rites of passage, symbolism, and tradition which that entails. Psychoanalysis, although offering a sophisticated esoteric practice to its patients, does not offer membership in an institution. This follows from the fact that the relationship is based around the medical model of illness. The assumption is that once the patient is cured, they no longer require the service. There is no lasting duty of care to the patient on the part of the psychoanalyst, except as the patient may relapse and require further attention.

We might be tempted to say that psychoanalysis does not offer a true Orphan-Elder relationship, but we must remember that psychoanalysis is part of the larger belief structure we have called science and technocracy. The choice to visit a psychoanalyst instead of a Christian priest already implies that the "patient" has been initiated into the belief structure of science and technocracy rather than the Christian religion. Therefore, we could still say that the psychoanalyst functions as an Elder who initiates Orphan into an institution where "institution" means a set of abstract beliefs that have not been made concrete and formal.

To say it again, the technocracy has little in the way of formal, exoteric structure. It exists primarily in the esoteric realm as a direct representation of the higher esoteric beliefs of the culture. The Elder has disappeared from Western culture in an exoteric sense in the same way that many of the institutions of our culture have become esoteric. Western culture has moved away from formally defined practices and belief structures towards ones that are informal, esoteric, and largely invisible. Our institutions run on ideology. It is the ephemeral nature of ideology that allows for the rapid changes in culture that we saw in the 20th century. But it also this rapid change that killed the Elder archetype. From an anthropological point of view, it is true that the expert fulfils the social functions required of the Elder. But from almost every other point of view, the Elder has disappeared. Most importantly, it has disappeared as an exoteric presence in our culture. Its representation in film and story is a pointer to the presence of the archetype in the collective unconscious, not as a live force in the cultural consciousness.

Crucially, this idea of a hidden or esoteric Elder is not some accidental or random occurrence. We can actually find it in the writings of two of the philosophers who have had a huge influence on these modern developments: John Locke and Jean-Jacques Rousseau. Rousseau in particular created a theory of education whereby the educator (Elder) should make themselves invisible. The student was to be guided towards fixed conclusions, but they must be made to think that they had discovered those conclusions themselves. This was not done out of spite or the desire to manipulate, but in the hope that it would encourage the student to find their own path later on. Liberalism's ethic of self-discovery and self-creation requires Elders to pretend that they are not there. This was explicitly built into the theory which motivated modern liberalism.

We see another expression of this underlying idea in one of the great romantic prophets of the 19th century. In the *Ring Cycle* of German composer Richard Wagner, the young Orphan, Siegfried, is silently watched and guided by the god, Wotan, culminating in a dramatic scene where the young man breaks the staff of the god, symbolising his coming of age. This is not a formal initiation. In fact, Siegfried does not know who Wotan is, since the god appears before him in disguise. Wotan is the model of Rousseau's educator who guides the initiate invisibly towards an outcome. Note that, in our terminology, Wotan is not just an Elder but a god. He is also an ancestor to Siegfried. Therefore, he fills all three archetypes we identified earlier – Elder, Ancestor, God/Spirit. One of the ideas that Wagner explores with his opera is the one we have already noted, that the gods have gone away and that it is now up to humans to create themselves. Again, we have the idea of the invisible Elder directly related to the twilight of the gods.

The resolution to our difficulties in analysis is that the West has esoteric Elders but not exoteric ones. This makes sense because every society must have a method of initiating the next generation. If we define the Elder role as whoever has responsibility for initiation, then we must say that the experts are the Elders of the modern technocracy. This works from an anthropological point of view. But from an archetypal point of view, we must conclude that the Elders and gods have gone away. This loss of the Elder was not an accidental occurrence but the logical outcome of philosophies that we have given the name of liberalism, which includes many of the romantic ideals of the 19th century. These quite explicitly renounced the Elder archetype in favour of "freedom" with the notion that the young should be left alone as much as possible to develop according to "nature".

As a final point on this difficult topic, let's return to the theme of this chapter. Remember, we have posited two archetypal pairs: the Child-Parent and the Orphan-Elder. The logic of these pairings says that if the Orphan-Elder relationship goes away, the Child-Parent pairing remains dominant. We saw a prime example of that with our case study on aristocratic women of the 19th century, where the inability to establish an Orphan-Elder relationship left those women stuck in the Child-Parent pair. Could that be a true also of modern Western culture? We have already shown one example where it is true and that is in the familial domain, where the dominance of the nuclear family has made the Grandparent role almost entirely redundant. The Child-Parent relationship has largely usurped the Child-Grandparent one in the family. Moreover, we have seen that the technocracy works through the Parents especially in the provision of education, healthcare, and mental health.

Could it be that this pattern extends beyond the family and into the broader socio-cultural domain? Is the dominance of the experts at the expense of the Elders a sign of a broader cultural trend where the Child-Parent relationship has become the model for social relations? Remember, an Elder's role is to initiate the Orphan and provide education and training that leads to a mature Adult identity. Experts do not do this. The expert is far more like the Parent in the sense that they demand obedience from the general public, who are assumed to be as ignorant as children and therefore require to be led rather than educated. It may very well be that the loss of the Elder offers only the "freedom" of the Child, which is to say, the freedom from responsibility, which is now placed solely in the hands of the expert who becomes the Parent in a Child-Parent relationship.

In one sense, of course, this dynamic is not new. It is, in fact, simply the difference between the elites of society and the general public, and the elites always have more power than the common folk. We might argue that the situation in the modern West is no different now than it was at the time of the Reformation, with the experts in the role of the Catholic clergy, wielding power over the general public. However, even if that is true, what is different about the two systems is that the form of dominance exercised by the modern technocratic elite is an esoteric and invisible one, whereas the Catholic Church's dominance was overt and exoteric. Put into the terms of this chapter, we would say that the Catholic Church governed via the Orphan-Elder pairing, while the modern technocracy exercises its dominance via the Child-Parent model.

This was the conclusion I had drawn in my book *The Devouring Mother: The Collective Unconscious in the Time of Corona*, although at the time I wrote that I had not yet realised the larger archetypal context at play. The technocracy's attitude towards the general public has come to mimic that of the Parent towards the Child. The technocracy is not interested in initiating the public but rather in controlling its behaviour. Alongside a number of other social trends, it really does seem that the experts are not proper replacements for the Elders and we conclude that the Orphan-Elder relationship has gone missing from the broader culture, leaving the Child-Parent pairing as the dominant template by which the elites of our society wield power over the general public.

Conclusion

We have had to spend a great deal of time in this chapter on the Orphan-Elder relationship in the modern West precisely because the complicated nature of that relationship in our culture has made both archetypes problematic. What we saw in the case of both the Elder in the 20th century and the aristocratic female Orphans of the 19th was that when the exoteric role gets taken away, this does not make the archetype itself null and void; rather, it exists in esoteric form only. The case of modern science is interesting in this respect since it is predicated, in many respects, on a rejection of the Elder. The Enlightenment thinkers truly believed that reason could set man free from arbitrary and oppressive authority. Translated into archetypal terms, they believed they could get rid of Elders. Nevertheless, science has ended up being shoehorned into something very like an Elder role. The psychological and anthropological need for the role did not go away just because we said it should.

The problematic nature of the Orphan-Elder relationship in the modern West ties back to the upheavals in the higher esoteric in the 19th and 20th centuries, which replaced the old Elders of the Christian church with the experts of technocracy and science. But we should also note that, even within the Christian religion, there was a movement away from the formal role of the Elder especially in the evangelical movement that also came to the fore in the 19th century. In turn, we can trace that development back to the Reformation's rejection of the role that had been the chief Elder for Western culture until that time: the Pope. The rejection of the Pope in the religious domain was followed by the rejection of the King in the political. Thus, the higher esoteric beliefs that form the core of modern Western culture—science, the Enlightenment, evangelical Protestantism, democracy, and liberalism— imply a rejection of Elders. The authority of the Elder was denied firstly at the religious-higher esoteric level of being and then later in the socio-cultural and, eventually, even the biological-familial. Once again, when we think through these issues from the point of view of the archetypes, seemingly unrelated social phenomena are seen to follow the same pattern: the rejection of the Elder.

It is natural that discussions of the Orphan-Elder relationship would veer off into some of the deeper questions of the higher esoteric because it is that pairing which is first and foremost about the initiation of the next generation into a culture. Meanwhile, we can think of the Child-Parent pairing as being primarily responsible for the biological propagation of society. Putting these together, we can use the archetypal pairs to map out the progression of the generations within a society or culture as follows:-

The gods/spirits						
Ancestor		Ancestor		Ancestor		
	Elder		Elder			
Adult/Parent		Adult/Parent		Adult/Parent		
	Orphan		Orphan			
Child		Child		Child		
Generation 1		Generation 2		Generation 3		

Although this chapter has focused heavily on developments in modern Western culture, we need to reiterate that the two archetypal pairings are universals of human society. Every culture must initiate the next generation and that initiation is done during the Orphan years of life. Even the modern West's attempt to get rid of the Elder has only pushed the archetype into the esoteric domain.

If we refocus now back on the core concept of this chapter, we began with the insight that the metamorphosis-stability pattern can also be extended to the archetypal pairs. The metamorphosis needs to be thought of not as an individual event that is short in duration but as a process that lasts over months or even years, during which the individual and the pair transition into their new identities. This process occurs across all three domains of identity: the biological, socio-cultural, and higher esoteric. We saw that the metamorphosis period is just as much about relinquishing the old identity as adapting to the new. This is especially true of the Orphan-Elder transition since the Child, Parent, and Elder metamorphoses must all be present to make it happen. The metamorphosis process ends when all individuals involved have settled into their new identities. There usually follows a long period of stability, but if the archetypal pair gets broken up either by external or internal issues, all parties are thrown back into a new metamorphosis.

This way of thinking about the archetypes and their relations has introduced a normative aspect into our model. It is fitting that this chapter addressed the arrival of psychoanalysis as a cultural force in the 20th century. What Freud and Jung did was to take the concept of illness from the medical domain and apply it to the psychic, bringing the issue of "mental health" to public consciousness. To a certain extent, we have made the same claim for our archetypology model. If the archetypes have a normative aspect to them, then a break in the archetypal pattern leads to pathology. But much like the body responds to a pathology by healing, it seems that individuals and even entire cultures respond to an archetypal pathology.

This use of medical concepts of health and illness is far more precise than it might appear at first glance. The archetypal metamorphosis period can be thought of as an illness from which we recover back to the stability of health. What's more, it is clear that cultures treat the metamorphosis in a very similar way to the treatment of illness. As we will see in the next chapter, it appears to be a universal of human society that the risks of the archetypal metamorphoses are mitigated by the administration of a variety of ceremonies and rites of passage to assist the individual through the difficult and risky period. Where those practices break down, as in the case of aristocratic women in the 19th century, something very much like illness tends to follow. We can call this "mental illness", but the esoteric manifestation is just a symptom of the archetypal pathology.

Another way to think about the same dynamic is via the concept of *initiation*. We have seen in this chapter that the Elder's role is to initiate the Orphans into the institutions of society. However, it is more broadly true that every archetype requires an initiation. There are two main methods that every society seems to use. The first is the rites of passage, the formal ceremonies which demarcate major turning points in life, e.g., baptisms, marriage ceremonies, and funerals. The second method of initiation is literature in the broadest sense of the word, including myths, legends, fairy tales, and stories. As Jung and his followers discovered, literature is full of archetypes. Stories are initiatory in the sense that they communicate the archetypal challenges to us and give us some idea of how we might surmount them in our own lives.

All of this leads to the theme that we will explore in the remainder of the book. Both rites of passage and stories are initiatory at a far deeper level than just their content. The very form of rites and stories, the underlying pattern which structures them, is identical to the pattern we have sketched out for the archetypal phases of life. Rites and stories can be thought of as a process in the same way that the archetypal metamorphosis is a process. What we find beneath the surface is a shared pattern that we will call the cycle-ending-in-transcendence. That will be the subject of the next chapter.

Chapter 4: The Cycle Ending in Transcendence

We have shown that the archetypal phases of life are punctuated by metamorphoses, intense periods of transition that signify the move from one archetype to the next. These metamorphoses can be thought of as resonating across the biological, socio-cultural, and higher esoteric levels of being. At the end of the last chapter, we noted that the socio-cultural metamorphoses take the form of rites and ceremonies that can be thought of as an initiation into the archetype itself. This is most clear in relation to the Orphan archetype since that it is the time in life when we must break from the family and be inducted into the institutions of society. However, these practices can be interpreted more broadly as the socio-cultural metamorphosis that ushers in the new archetypal phase. The purpose of this is not just to assist the individual through the difficult metamorphosis period, it is to signal to the wider community that a change of state has taken place.

Thus, the metamorphoses that mark the beginning of each archetype resonate differently at the various levels of being. The biological metamorphosis is always a personal affair in that a specific individual must go through it. The socio-cultural metamorphosis incorporates the wider society. Sometimes, as in the case of birth, pregnancy, or death, the socio-cultural metamorphosis is synchronous with the biological one. However, there are also times when the socio-cultural metamorphosis can be held earlier or later than the biological one. The initiation of Orphans is an example of a socio-cultural metamorphosis that follows the biological one (puberty). The time differential between the two can be many years. Meanwhile, marriage is an example where the socio-cultural transition is expected to come before the biological one (childbirth). In all cases, however, the socio-cultural rite is there to give structure and assistance to the biological metamorphosis. It is also there as the expression of the higher esoteric beliefs of the culture. We have mentioned an example from modern Western history, where the rites of the Christian faith have been swapped for the belief structure of reason and science.

The crucial point, however, is that even though the belief structure of the higher esoteric may change, the archetypes remain the same, and so does the timing of the socio-cultural metamorphosis. This makes sense because the archetypal phases of life are grounded in biology. Thus, whether marriage takes place in a church (Christian belief structure) or a registrar's office (technocracy), it still typically takes place prior to the birth of a child. The same is true for the socio-cultural metamorphoses around birth, puberty, and death.

Because the archetypes are grounded in biology, the socio-cultural practices around them are universals of human culture. We owe the knowledge about the universality of such rites to the golden age of comparative scholarship that occurred in the 19th and early 20th centuries in Europe. The global reach of European civilisation in the 19th century allowed for the cataloguing of the various rituals and ceremonies practiced by numerous different societies. What this revealed was that every culture has a set of major rites that mark the archetypal metamorphoses. The Belgian anthropologist Arnold van Gennep called these *rites of passage.*

Van Gennep's work is crucial for our analysis because it was based on an extensive cross-cultural survey. He identified rites around pregnancy and birth (the Parent archetype), childhood (Child archetype), initiation (Orphan archetype), marriage (Adult archetype), and death (Elder/Ancestor). The kinds of rites that are used and the cultural significance attached to them can differ greatly, of course. A tribal initiation given to the Orphans of a hunter-gatherer community differs in many respects from the Catholic rite of Confirmation given to the Orphans of medieval Europe, which differs again from the Bar Mitzvah given to Jewish Orphans. What they all have in common, however, is that they mark the beginning of the Orphan phase of life. The same is true for marriage ceremonies, birth and death rituals, and rituals around pregnancy and childbirth. They are all socio-cultural ceremonies that map directly to an archetypal metamorphosis.

That insight from van Gennep would already have been invaluable as empirical justification for the model of archetypology we have built up so far. But van Gennep's work provides a second crucial result whose significance will ground our analysis for the rest of the book. What he found was that the rites of passage, the ceremonial and ritual practices from around the world that correspond to what we have called socio-cultural metamorphoses, have a universal structure to them. The content of the rites of passage and the higher esoteric belief structures to which they correspond can vary enormously, but the underlying pattern is the same. Just as we have gone looking for the underlying patterns beneath the archetypal phases of life in this book, van Gennep went looking for the pattern that unified the rites of passage. Crucially, what he found was the same pattern we have identified for the archetypes.

In van Gennep's terminology, the rites of passage are invocations of what a culture holds to be *sacred*. Not only does this concept of sacredness have obvious parallels to what we have called the higher esoteric domain, but it also ties back directly to the concepts of health and illness and therefore to the biological level of being. In other words, the rites of passage can also be analysed using our three levels of being: the biological, socio-cultural, and higher esoteric.

Because of these clear correspondences between the rites of passage and the archetypes, we can use van Gennep's analysis to expand our archetypal framework. That is what we will be doing in this chapter. In addition to his anthropological viewpoint, we will also utilise the work of another famous comparative scholar from the 20th century. We said at the end of the last chapter that there were two initiatory devices that societies use to handle the archetypal metamorphoses. Van Gennep's rites of passage are one, and the other is literature and myth. It was Joseph Campbell who investigated the underlying structure of myth and found the exact same structure that van Gennep had identified for rites. He called it the h*ero's journey.*

What all this means is that the two main practices that every culture uses as initiation to the archetypal phases of life have the same structure as the archetypes themselves. There is an underlying unity at play. We will spend the rest of the book working our way towards an understanding of that unity.

The Rites of Passage

At the core of our analysis of the archetypes has been the transition between metamorphosis and stability. We have showed that the metamorphosis takes place across the three levels of being. For example, the biological metamorphosis of pregnancy must be accompanied by the socio-cultural metamorphosis that establishes the family unit that is concerned with the care of the Child. All of this must be backed up by the higher esoteric metamorphosis in the individuals who accept the new responsibilities that come from the archetypal roles they are moving into. At any of these levels of being, there may be problems. In fact, there are guaranteed to be problems because a reconfiguration of one's identity is a big deal. The metamorphosis period ends when the new identity has been established and solidified. That doesn't mean that there can't be further problems afterwards, it just means that the part of the process that is about accepting the new archetypal identity is over.

What van Gennep found with the rites of passage is that they follow the exact same pattern of a difficult transition period between stable states. For him, every rite of passage is about a transition between *profane* and *sacred* status. There can be all kinds of different rites of passage, including ones that mark major life events like birth, pregnancy, and death, but they all share this underlying structure. To go through a rite of passage is to become sacred. To come out the other side is to return to profane status. Just as our metamorphosis is a time of heightened risk, so too is the sacred status of the initiate in a rite of passage. The rite of passage is there to allow the initiate to navigate the difficulty. At this point, it is worth spending some time understanding the meanings of the words sacred and profane, as these are not terms we understand well in our secular and materialist culture.

The word *sacred* means to make holy. The word *holy* is in turn related to the words *whole* and *health*. To be unholy is to be un-whole and unhealthy. To make sacred is to return to wholeness, health, and holiness. Although we return to the state of wholeness after the sacred process is completed, it is not exactly true to say we are the same. Rather, the sacred process is an exchange. There must be a sacrifice. We sacrifice something, but we get something in return. That is why the journey from the profane to the sacred and back is a journey of transformation or metamorphosis. The rites of passage are there to facilitate a metamorphosis that is dangerous because it requires us to become un-whole, unholy, and unhealthy for a time. Rites of passage are sacred because they are the process which allows us to transform ourselves.

Since we return to the same state in which we started, we can model the rites of passage as a cycle. Van Gennep divided the cycle into three phases, which he called *separation, transition,* and *incorporation.* We can show these on a simple diagram as follows:-

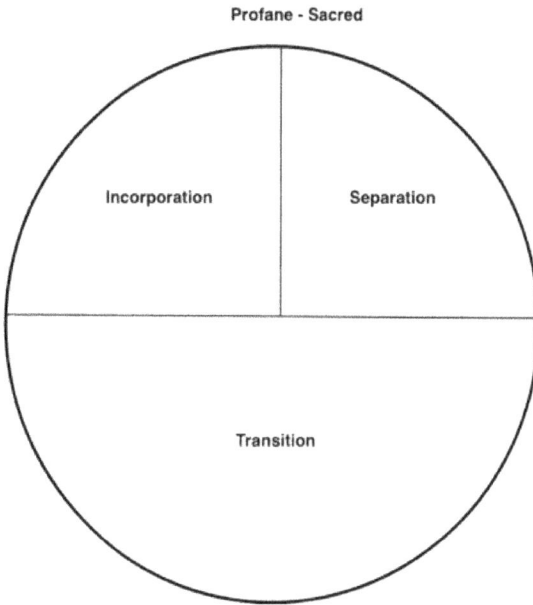

The separation phase is about disconnecting from the normal, everyday world and stepping into the sacred world in which the rite will take place. Religious buildings of all kinds fulfil this purpose by definition because they are sacred, but any building or space that is distinct from normal life can fit the bill. This is especially true when the building has some kind of protection from the everyday world. Religious buildings provide spiritual protection, but buildings such as parliament houses, science laboratories, and army barracks can also be included since they all have formal rules for access and punishments for breaking the rules. The formality of sacred spaces also includes special dress requirements, specific times of access, official roles for those who staff the building, and strict behaviour codes. All of these mark the space as distinct from normal life. The purpose is to create the feeling of separateness from the everyday world and thereby to facilitate the rite of passage. Thus, even nominally secular societies and institutions fit within van Gennep's concept of the sacred.

Once all the participants of the ritual have detached from their everyday lives and are physically and mentally in the sacred space, the transition phase of the rite begins. We can think of this phase as the one which elaborates on the specific version of sacredness that the rite deals with. It would include introductions on the part of the leaders of the rite who explain to those present why they are there and what is the meaning of the occasion. It introduces the main participants and sets the expectations for their performance. In a lengthy and high-stakes rite of passage, this phase would also include training and testing of the initiate's capability. There could be other physical and mental challenges such as hazing rites or tests of courage. If the rite is structured in such a way as to be a genuine test of the initiate, it is the transition phase where we would expect to see people drop out due to a failure to meet the challenges they are confronted with.

Finally, the incorporation phase is synonymous with the overall purpose of the rite. For example, the purpose of a marriage rite is to join two people together in matrimony. The actions which are taken to signify that this is now the case take place in the incorporation phase of the ceremony. The same is true of all other rites. The initiate is now assumed to have passed the test or met the minimum requirements expected of them. They still need to complete the final section of the rite successfully, but the incorporation phase is about the main participants signifying that they accept the new status that the rite bestows on them and the institution accepting that the initiate deserves to have that new status bestowed. At the end of the incorporation phase, the initiate is no longer an initiate but has graduated to the new status that the rite confers on them.

To better understand the meaning of the three segments, let's walk through an analysis of the traditional Western marriage ceremony as an example.

The church building is the sacred space that is already demarcated from the everyday world by its grand architecture and internal ambience. Formal clothing is a requirement for all observers of the ceremony, but there are even more formal requirements for the participants, especially the two main initiates: the bride and groom. Formal behaviour is also expected of the general attendees, while the behaviour of the main participants—the bride, father of the bride, groom, best man, and priest—is almost entirely defined in advance and needs to be practiced for that reason.

Walking through each of van Gennep's three phases, we can see that the separation phase of the rite begins when an individual creates a (sacred) space for the event. That is the time when you accept the invitation and mark it in your calendar. Getting dressed in your formal clothes and making your way to the sacred location is also part of the separation phase. Since this is not a part of your normal routine, it removes you from the pattern of everyday life. The separation phase ends when you are inside the sacred space and ready to perform whatever role is assigned to you. Once everybody is inside and ready, the transition phase begins.

For a traditional Western wedding, that is signalled by the entry of the bride and father of the bride. This begins the formal part of the proceeding. All behaviour during this phase is strictly governed by ceremonial requirements. It is because of the specific nature of the behaviour required that there is a heightened sense of risk for the participants. For formal events, that risk is mostly social in nature, such as making a mistake that will be remembered in the future. Some level of risk is required in order for an event to be sacred. You are exposed and incomplete, out on a limb and needing to find your way back. The way back may be laid out for you, but you still must rise to the occasion and perform your part correctly. Thus, we have the well-known stories of those who fail to fulfil their role including the best man who loses the ring or the groom who forgets his lines.

The transition part of a traditional Christian marriage ceremony would include a prayer and a short sermon by the priest on the subject of matrimony. This leads to the incorporation phase, which is the business end of any rite of passage. It's the part that formalises the overall purpose of the rite. In this case, the purpose is to marry two people. Thus, the incorporation phase includes the wedding vows, the exchanging of rings, the famous words, "I now pronounce you man and wife," and the kiss, which quite literally brings two bodies together *in corporeal*. The physical incorporation of the kiss is symbolic of the legal incorporation of the couple in marriage and is followed by their incorporation into a single household. As the traditional wedding vows make clear, this incorporation may only be severed by death; at least, that's the way it used to be.

Within this template of separation, transition, and incorporation, a practically infinite number of rites of passage can be created in just the same way that the rules of language allow for an infinite number of expressions to be written or spoken. Rites of passage differ not just by the cultural content associated with the belief structure being conveyed but also by the level of performance expected of the initiate. Wedding ceremonies do not require much because the rite is designed to be passed by every member of society. But for institutions where an elite standard of performance is required, the rites of passage that govern entry can be extreme. Examples include esoteric religious institutions, elite sports, and military and political institutions. Even in these more extreme cases, however, the rite of passage still follows the separation, transition, and incorporation pattern that van Gennep identified.

We noted earlier that a true rite of passage requires a sacrifice. You must give something up in order to get something in return. Marriage is a good example of this because you give up the possibility of marrying any other person in order to marry just this one person. You give up the benefits of single life for married life. You give up freedom and autonomy for the chance to start a family. You give up the opportunities open to the Orphan and accept the responsibilities of the Adult.

Because rites of passage are socio-cultural ceremonies, they also function to signal to the rest of society that a status change has taken place. All those who were present at the wedding ceremony now know that you are married. Those who weren't present can see it from the ring on your finger. Rites of passage confer new forms of address on the initiate, new legal statuses, new economic and political rewards, and a variety of other tangible and publicly visible markers that the initiate did not have before. It follows from this that a rite of passage is a metamorphosis not just at an individual level but at a social one.

This latter fact is crucial because it pertains to the distinction we have been making throughout the book between the exoteric and the esoteric. Although rites of passage embody and communicate the higher esoteric beliefs of the culture, and although they are designed to evoke a strong esoteric response in the participants, ultimately, a rite of passage is about the exoteric and formal process. For example, it is possible to go through the rite of marriage without feeling any emotional connection to one's marriage partner or even to believe that the ceremony itself is valid. This level of cynicism is not uncommon in the world. What it shows is that the successful completion of a rite does not require one's heart to be in it, only that one complete the actions required. That is what we mean when we say that the rites are primarily exoteric, although, of course, the ideal scenario is that the initiate really does believe in the rite and experiences it esoterically as well.

In summary, the major rites of passage of society are there to guide us through the metamorphosis required to transition from one archetype to the other. The main way in which the rites help the individual through the metamorphosis period is by signalling to society that the metamorphosis has occurred. In the modern world, we are familiar with the concept of *peer pressure*, which is normally used in a pejorative sense of being tempted into something that is not good for you. But peer pressure can be used for good to the extent that society encourages your behaviour in a positive direction. The rites of passage create that positive pressure by signalling a change of identity so that others will begin to treat you as if you had already attained it. For individuals struggling with issues of self-belief tied to an archetypal metamorphosis, it surely must help if others begin treating them as if they were worthy of the archetype in question. To use some more modern vernacular, the rites of passage encourage you to *fake it until you make it.*

But this strength of the rites of passage can also be a weakness. The fact that rites can be faked means that individuals who do not believe in them can nevertheless receive the social status conferred by the rite. If this becomes a habit, both the rites and the institutions which guard them can become corrupt. We can understand this corruption by using our esoteric-exoteric distinction. The rites of passage imply the higher esoteric beliefs of a culture. They are symbols of those beliefs. If the rite becomes corrupted, it means that the initiate is not required to believe in the higher esoteric symbols. In that case, their initiation has taken place in the socio-cultural domain only. Thus, we say that institutional corruption occurs when the rites of passage no longer initiate individuals into the higher esoteric. The higher esoteric and the socio-cultural realms diverge as a result.

To understand the ramifications of this divergence, we can use the life story of a man who experienced such institutional corruption as an existential crisis: Martin Luther.

A Case Study on Luther

To understand the story of Luther, we are able to draw on the hard work we have done up to this point in relation to the Orphan-Elder relationship. Rites of passage are initiations that are always carried out by Elders. This is true even when the initiate is not in the Orphan phase of life. For a traditional Western marriage ceremony, for example, the priest is the Elder who represents the institution of the church. It is the church which has the power to confer on the initiates (bride and groom) the new social statuses that they will have at the completion of the rite. In fact, we can add this property to our definition of the Elder archetype: an Elder is the representative of an institution whose role is to conduct the rites of passage governing the entry of initiates (remembering that we are using *institution* in the broader sense to include informal practices).

Sometimes the institution that the Elder represents is a small and local affair, perhaps a tribe in a hunter-gatherer society or a small club or association in modern society. Sometimes, however, the institution is big and complex and spans a wide geographical area. In that case, there is usually a local Elder who administers to the community and a hierarchy of Elders with a representative at the top of the tree who is responsible for the management of the whole institution. One of history's most pertinent examples of such a hierarchical and geographically dispersed institution was the one that was dominant during Luther's time. The Catholic Church had an extensive network of Elders (priests) all over Europe led by the highest-ranking Elder in Rome, the Pope.

One of the features of large hierarchical institutions is that, although new Orphan initiates are inducted by somebody lower down the tree, they are brought under the authority of the highest Elder, since that individual has power over the entire organisation. In relation to the Catholic Church, this fact is taken for granted. Although initiates are inducted into a local church, it is the Pope who is the supreme leader and to whom fealty is owed. In such cases, there is a kind of dual Orphan-Elder relationship that is formed, a direct one with the Elder who carries out the initiation and training, and a more symbolic one with the Elder who leads the institution.

Thus, when Luther joined a monastery in northern Germany, he would have been given an initiation rite of passage by the local head of the monastery, who would have made it clear that the ultimate allegiance was to the Pope in Rome. Because Luther was joining as a monk, he was on a pathway to becoming what we have called a religious elite (Sage archetype), and that would have meant a more intensive rite of passage focused on esoteric religious discipline. The training given to Luther was rigorous and lengthy and included intense practices such as self-flagellation.

It is clear that Luther expressly desired such a rigorous esoteric initiation. In fact, his desires exceeded what was required. The demands of the training weren't enough for him, and he pushed himself much harder than the others. Luther's problem seemed to be that he required more esoteric stimulus than the rites of passage typically imparted. That was bad enough, but Luther also saw a lot of corruption around him. Many of his peers were openly lazy and cynical, and, perhaps most importantly, the church seemed to have corrupted its ideals, for example, by engaging in the production of goods and services for profit.

All of this came to a head with Luther's journey to Rome. While the corruption he saw at a local level could have been attributed to a small sub-section of the church, the Italian trip made him realise that it was not an anomaly. The worldliness of the church was on full display in Rome, and the popes of that era were not in any way shy of showing off their luxuriance and, from Luther's point of view, debauchery. As a result, Luther's gripes against his local church Elders turned into a gripe against the supreme Elder – the Pope.

In one sense, Luther's charge against the church was one that could be made against any institution throughout history. Institutions are in a constant battle against corruption, and many of them do not win that battle and can fall into long periods of decadence. There is little doubt that the Catholic Church in Luther's time was in a state of hyper-decadence. Luther was not the only one to notice.

But we can be more specific about what this means. It means that the exoteric and esoteric are out of alignment. The institution does not practice what it preaches. Luther believed that the church should be concerned solely with spiritual matters, and yet it was clearly involved in worldly affairs such as economics, politics, and even military disputes. In his eyes, the religious rites of passage of the church had become degraded because the church was really pursuing a different mission. For Luther, this was a betrayal of the esoteric meaning of the religion. Thus, the problem was not that the exoteric rites of passage didn't exist; it was that the church no longer really believed in those rites. The rites had become exoteric only; empty ceremonies. They were being conducted under false pretences since the proceeds of the church's operations were being used to fund activities that had nothing to do with the faith. Luther's personal dissatisfaction at the lack of esoteric meaning in the rites that he went through turned into a general charge against the church.

Rites of passage are a metamorphosis at the exoteric, social level that are also supposed to evoke a metamorphosis at the esoteric, personal level. When there is a mismatch between the two, it can be due either to the institution itself, or it can be an issue with the individual. Luther would easily have passed his training and become a monk. He more than exceeded the standard required by the church. Yet, he could not really believe in those rites. He found no esoteric meaning there. The fact that the church would have accepted him anyway only made him despise the institution more because he did not believe himself to be at the standard that he thought should apply to a true believer.

Perhaps an analogy with modern sports can help elucidate how Luther felt. Imagine there's a sports team that has a reputation as being the best of the best. A young man dreams of one day becoming a member of the team. He trains as hard as he can and builds up his skills, knowing that only the best can get in. Finally, he gets to try out for the team, and is accepted, only to find out once he's on the inside that things are nothing like what he imagined.

His teammates are lazy and cynical. His coach clearly couldn't care less. The owner of the team (highest-ranking Elder) doesn't even pay attention but is off doing other things that have nothing to do with the sport. In general, all the young man finds is corruption and decadence. In this case, we say that the team exists exoterically, since it still has its reputation as the best of the best. But esoterically, it has ceased to exist. It has lost its spirit.

In other circumstances, Luther's disgust at the hypocrisy and corruption of the church could have resulted in him simply renouncing his faith and finding something else to do. That is always the most likely scenario because institutions have a numerical and political advantage over individuals. In the case of the Catholic Church, that advantage had been put to good use over the centuries with numerous heretics put to death. Luther seemed destined for the same fate, but, like many other religious figures throughout history, his critique of the church and his self confidence was grounded in his belief that he had his own mandate from the higher esoteric. Luther claimed to have God on his side, and with that esoteric assurance, he sought to reconfigure the exoteric structure of the church itself.

What we see in the case of Luther is a man who had attained an exoteric identity via completing rites of passage but who was not esoterically fulfilled. This is a different scenario to the origins of the feminist movement which we traced to the absence of exoteric identity altogether. Nevertheless, what both have in common is an imbalance between the exoteric and esoteric aspects of identity. What they also have in common is that the problem manifested during the Orphan phase of life. That is not a coincidence because it is at this stage of life that we are initiated into both the socio-cultural institutions of society and also the higher esoteric beliefs of the culture. Young people feel the decadence of institutions more acutely than those who have become accustomed to it. Luther thought he was joining an institution dedicated to the pursuit of the spiritual but he found one that was more concerned with money and power. His disillusionment was not primarily with the rites of passage, which still claimed to be symbols of the sacred, but with the Elders who administered those rites, since they did not manifest the higher esoteric beliefs which the rites referred to. Thus, the case of Luther is another example of the breakdown of the Orphan-Elder relationship. But, in his case, the breakdown was caused not by the absence of rites but by the mismatch between the rites and the higher esoteric beliefs, i.e., institutional corruption.

The story of Luther helps us to understand where the rites of passage fit within our archetypal model. Rites of passage are initiations. They belong to what we have called the archetypal metamorphosis phase, where they facilitate the initiate's induction into the socio-cultural institutions of society, with the corresponding higher esoteric belief structure that motivates those institutions. In Luther we have the rare case of an individual who sees that the rites of passage have become empty ceremonies brokered by a corrupt institution whose stated mission no longer corresponds with its actions. As a result, the rites of passage that he went through had become devoid of higher esoteric meaning. Luther correctly held the Elders of the church (priest, bishop, and pope) responsible for this since it is the Elders of society who are responsible for guarding and propagating the belief structure and the integrity of the institutions which uphold it. It is the Elders who must ensure that the rites of passage have meaning for the Orphans who are being initiated.

In the case of Luther, the corruption in the rites of passage was part of a larger breakdown in the Orphan-Elder relationship in the society of his time. This causes an archetypal crisis in the same way that the similar breakdown in the 19th century caused the crisis that gave birth to feminism. Luther's personal archetypal crisis tapped into the larger problem of corruption with the Catholic Church. Thus, the Reformation can also be seen as a response to an archetypal pathology. When institutions become corrupt, the Orphan-Elder relationship breaks down. This creates pressure to fix the problem. One way to do this is to swap the Elders with ones who still believe in the esoteric mission of the institution. Another way is to abandon the institution and start a competing one. History shows a surprisingly common third option, which is that nothing gets done and both the institution and the larger culture of which it is a part slowly atrophy until they are conquered from without.

In the case of the Protestants, what happened was a new set of institutions was created, i.e., the various Protestant denominations. But these institutions had a peculiar feature, one that is crucial to an understanding of modern

Western culture. Not only did the Protestants reject the Elders of the Catholic Church and the rites of passage that they conducted, but they also rejected all Elders and all rites of passage in favour of a direct esoteric connection between the worshipper and God. From an archetypology point of view, the Protestants denied the Orphan-Elder relationship altogether. It is largely because of them that we have ended up in the strange situation we have in the modern West of denying the Elder role.

In the case of Luther, this was not just a churlish move motivated by the anti-authoritarian impulse of youth. The reason why Luther was sensitive to the fact that the exoteric rites of the church were no longer in alignment with its stated esoteric purpose was because he had experienced a connection with the higher esoteric prior to joining the monastery. It was the confidence that this experience instilled that led him to take on the most powerful institution in Europe at that time. Within our model of archetypology, we say that Luther had experienced an esoteric metamorphosis that had no corresponding exoteric component. In order to account for this, we need a concept that can explain esoteric metamorphosis in its own terms, and we find exactly that in another great work of comparative scholarship from the 20th century.

Remember we said earlier that societies have two primary forms of initiation. The rites of passage are the first. The second is myth and story. Just as van Gennep found the underlying pattern to the rites of passage via his comparative anthropology, another scholar in the 20th century found an identical pattern to myth and story. His name was Joseph Campbell, and he called his pattern *the hero's journey.*

The Hero's Journey as Esoteric Metamorphosis

Van Gennep arrived at the rites of passage pattern after an exhaustive cross-cultural study of ceremony and ritual. Joseph Campbell arrived at the hero's journey by a similarly exhaustive cross-cultural study of mythology. Modern scholarship divides anthropology and mythology into discrete fields of study. However, from our point of view, the rites of passage and the hero's journey are tightly related. Both are initiatory devices, or, to say the same thing a different way, both are about metamorphoses.

This fact was known at least as early as the 4th century AD. The scholar Sallustius gave the name of *mixed myth* to the set of stories that were explicitly used in initiation. This is actually a quite obvious and uncontroversial idea once we learn to see it. All of the rites of passage conducted by the Christian church have their meaning supplemented and enhanced by the story of Jesus and from the Bible more broadly. A Christian mass includes both formal, ceremonial acts and readings from the Bible. Therefore, a Christian mass utilises *mixed myth* in the way that Sallustius meant. Its rites of passage (ceremonies) and its hero's journeys (stories, myths) work together to initiate the faithful.

We see the same thing in very different cultures. In Australian Aboriginal society, the boy going through initiation is taught the stories of the culture heroes of his tribe. Those stories, sometimes given the name of *songlines*, allow for a retracing of the steps of the journey gone through by the ancestors. The physical actions of the initiate (the rite of passage) get their meaning from the mythical journey told in the story.

The vital point to grasp is that these correspondences are not accidental, but fundamental. The underlying structure is the same for rites of passage and for hero's journeys. Whereas van Gennep analysed the rite of passage as a process of moving through the sacred and back to the profane, Campbell was influenced by the work of Carl Jung and gave his model a psychoanalytic focus. For him, the hero's journey was the process of moving out of consciousness, into the unconscious, and back. Campbell also analysed three discrete phases of the process, which he called *departure, initiation,* and *return.* Thus, we can represent the hero's journey on an identical diagram to the one we showed earlier for the rites of passage.

Conscious - Unconscious

Act 3: Return

Act 1: Departure

Act 2: Initiation

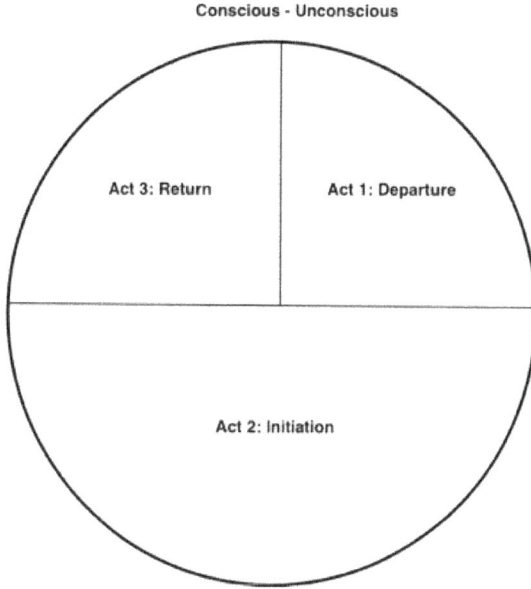

In Campbell's analysis, the hero of the story descends into the unconscious world, where they retrieve a prize that is incorporated into consciousness during the return phase of the story. The unconscious is often symbolised by strange, otherworldly phenomena that confront the hero with unpleasant realities that they would rather not deal with. The beautiful princess meets a grubby frog or an ugly troll. The warrior comes upon a group of witches in a misty forest. The ruler is confronted at midnight by a ghost or a strange character in a dream. The hero's journey is about getting up the courage to confront the unpleasant aspects of existence. In a Jungian sense, it is the process of *individuation*, where something unconscious and unknown must be integrated into consciousness. This inherently psychological way of framing the process makes clear that the hero's journey is the esoteric counterpart to the rites of passage. This makes sense because a story can convey inner experiences in far more detail than a rite of passage can.

A second correspondence between rites of passage and the hero's journeys is that they both congregate around the archetypal metamorphoses, which is exactly what we would expect given that both are initiatory devices. When we look for our four primary archetypes, as well as the sub-archetypes of Warrior, Ruler, Sage etc., we find that every hero in a hero's journey fits into one of them. For example, if we limit ourselves just to Shakespeare's greatest stories, we find that not only is every hero of the story a perfect example of one of our archetypes, but that the drama in the story comes from the fact that the hero is undergoing an archetypal metamorphosis, i.e., moving from one archetype to another. Since most of Shakespeare's famous stories are tragedies, they are, in fact, about the failure of the metamorphosis.

Romeo and Juliet are both Orphans who are trying to become Adults. We see that their marriage, which should be the socio-cultural rite of passage that successfully marks their entry to the Adult archetype, happens in secret. A secret marriage is an esoteric rite of passage that has no exoteric meaning because it is not recognised by the wider society. Romeo and Juliet have successfully attained the Adult archetype in an esoteric sense, but not an exoteric one. Their death is the result of a mismatch between the role they esoterically desire and the one their society exoterically demands of them.

The exact same dynamic holds in *Hamlet*, where the relationship between the young prince and Ophelia is scuttled by the meddling of their parents. Hamlet's famous line "Get thee to a nunnery" can be seen as an instruction to Ophelia to escape a hopeless situation and choose a different life path. Of course, she does not follow his suggestion, and both she and Hamlet fail in their Orphan mission to become Adults.

It is worth noting here that three of Shakespeare's comedies feature a successful Orphan to Adult transition. *A Midsummer Night's Dream*, *The Taming of the Shrew,* and *Much Ado About Nothing* all show us the love affair/marriage of their heroes.

Returning to the tragedies, the story of Othello is particularly interesting since it shows us a man who has attained worldly success as a great military leader. In this respect, Othello has already metamorphosed into the Warrior archetype. With his marriage to Desdemona, however, he is called on to become a Husband and to develop his familial identity. It is this which he fails to do. He is a man who has spent too long fighting enemies on the battlefield. When he brings the Warrior's mentality to his marriage (encouraged by his fellow soldier, Iago), it destroys both him and his wife.

Finally, we have the two tragedies which detail the failure of the Elder metamorphosis. This is most obvious in the case of King Lear, who is retiring from active service and handing over his kingdom to his daughters and their husbands. Macbeth is also called on to retire from the field of battle and take up the Elder role of thane offered to him by his king, Duncan. Both men fail in their mission because they are unable to let go of their past identity. Macbeth, like Othello, is the great Warrior who, when he has no external adversaries left, turns his friends and family into enemies so that he has somebody to fight. Meanwhile, Lear does not really want to give up power, as evidenced by the fact that he keeps a hundred soldiers with him. He is unable to relinquish his identity as Ruler. When his daughters have to forcibly remove him from power, his own tyrannical ways come back to bite him. Both his kingdom and his family are destroyed as a result.

The story of Lear mirrors the set of tragedies written by the ancient Greek writer Sophocles. *Oedipus the King* is about the monarch's Elder metamorphosis. Meanwhile, *Oedipus at Colonus* is about the hero's transition from Elder to Ancestor. The third of the so-called Theban Plays is about Antigone's transition from Orphan (literally, because her father has just died) to Adult.

We could continue to list famous stories which follow these patterns, but the point should be clear. Just as the rites of passage cluster around the archetypal transition points, so too do the greatest and most memorable of stories. They do so because the archetypal metamorphoses are the periods of highest danger and therefore provide a natural backdrop for great drama. But such myths and stories are also initiatory devices whose role is to show us the risks involved so that we may understand and identify them when we go through the same metamorphosis in our own lives.

Now, we have been focusing on the subset of rites and hero's journeys which deals with what we are calling initiation and metamorphosis. These are the major rites and stories in any society. But there are countless others that deal with more minor aspects of life. We can tell a story about event, no matter how banal, and as long as it fulfils the three-part structure outlined above, then it is a hero's journey. Similarly, every culture has numerous minor rites of passage that fulfil a number of low-level functions such as blessings, purification rituals, and feasts (even a family meal counts as a rite of passage). Even these more minor rites and stories follow the same pattern of a three-part cycle containing separation, transition, and incorporation phases. The unifying thread in all cases is that the cycle must contain a sacrifice. Sometimes the sacrifice is small, sometimes it is life changing.

This gives us another way to interpret the Shakespeare tragedies mentioned above because the sacrifice made by all of the heroes is, eventually, their own life. But before that major sacrifice, there are a number of sacrifices that are tied directly to the archetypal phase they are going through. King Lear tries to give up his kingdom. Macbeth and Othello try to give up the battlefield. Romeo, Juliet, and Hamlet try to give up their families. In all of these cases, the sacrifice the hero tries and fails to make is the exact sacrifice they should make based on our earlier analysis of the archetypes. Romeo, Juliet, and Hamlet are all Orphans. The Orphan is supposed to sacrifice the familial domain in order to find their identity outside of it. Othello is newly married. He is supposed to sacrifice his work to spend time with his wife. Macbeth and King Lear are Adults trying to transition into the Elder archetype. They are supposed to retire from active duty and take up a role as mentor or guide. In every one of these cases, the hero fails the archetypal transition because they fail to make the appropriate sacrifice. They transition into the sacred but never make it out the other side. We see the same thing in many of the original Brothers Grimm fairy tales, where the hero comes to a gruesome end meant as a warning to children about the dangers of the hero's journey.

Putting all this together, we can see that the initiatory rites of passage and hero's journeys share the same three-part cyclical structure consisting of separation, transition, and incorporation phases. They share the property that a sacrifice is required of the initiate/hero. They share the idea that this sacrifice really is a sacrifice; it really is a danger to the hero/initiate. And they share the fact that on the other side of the journey, the hero has undergone a metamorphosis.

But, of course, the key point is not just that the structure of rites and stories is the same, which would be of nothing more than academic interest. The key point is that we ourselves go through these processes. These are the lived experiences that we go through when we are initiated into each archetypal phase of life. When we get married, we are following the three-part cyclical structure of the rite of passage. We are sacrificing the opportunity to marry any other person in order to marry just this one person. We are sacrificing the benefits of single life for the opportunity to start a family. When we do these things, our society confers on us the new status of being married. In the modern world, that comes with a number of legal and financial benefits and responsibilities. In short, we have gone through a socio-cultural metamorphosis.

In relation to the hero's journeys, these are something that we all go through, but the difference is that the hero's journey is about the inner, esoteric experience. A marriage ceremony is a rite of passage. A story told about a marriage ceremony is a hero's journey. If a bride or groom tells the story of their own marriage, they may give us some idea of the actions that happened, but they will almost certainly focus the story on their feelings and emotions on the day and their general subjective perspective on the event. Now, this raises a crucial point. A more or less random set of impressions and subjective feelings is not a hero's journey because a hero's journey requires a sacrifice. Something must be on the line from the subjective, esoteric point of view. That's why the best marriage stories are usually ones where something went horribly wrong and the whole thing looked like it wasn't going to happen, but then someone saved it at the last minute. In that case, the sacrifice in the story was the potential failure of the marriage ceremony and the actions of the hero(es) to make it happen despite the difficulties.

A hero's journey must always be about the esoteric metamorphosis of the hero. This is different from the rites of passage, which are always primarily an exoteric metamorphosis. There is no way to fake an esoteric metamorphosis. You either have it or you don't. Of course, it is possible to pretend you have had one. Many religious frauds over the millennia have done so. But even then the fraud only works exoterically; it only works if people believe it and accord you the corresponding social status. A true hero's journey is about the subjective, esoteric side of metamorphosis. Think of how well we know Macbeth, Romeo, Juliet, Hamlet, Othello, and King Lear by the end of their stories. What they do in the story is of secondary importance. What is of primary importance is the esoteric metamorphosis they go through, which is a revelation of their character. The strange fact about hero's journeys is that they may be just as much of a surprise to the hero as they are to the audience. Even in our own lives, we may react to an event in a way that we didn't know we were capable of. The event changes our own perception of ourselves. This is what Joseph Campbell was talking about when he said the hero's journey is a journey into the unconscious. We learn something about ourselves that we didn't know. We incorporate it into consciousness.

It is this last point which touches on the most important difference between the rites of passage and the hero's journey. To say it one more time, the rites of passage are exoteric. The exoteric relates to the objective, tangible, visible world. We can analyse a marriage, or a baptism, or an Orphan initiation, or any other rite of passage according to the actions that are carried out. There may be any number of important symbolic meanings that require deeper levels of understanding, but the rites of passage are based in the external world and have a base level of objectivity as a result.

The esoteric nature of the hero's journeys makes them inherently subjective. What we have called the esoteric includes the full range of inner experiences that we may have. The easiest ones to understand are those that exist at the biological and socio-cultural levels of being. This includes feelings of tiredness, hunger, and cold at the biological level and feelings of anxiety, shame, or embarrassment at the socio-cultural. What all of these have in common is that they are immediate responses that we experience at the time when they happen. It is possible that the feeling lingers, especially in relation to shame and embarrassment, but feelings and emotions usually have a short shelf life.

Above these dimensions of the esoteric is the level of being we have called the higher esoteric. It is at the higher esoteric where the resonance of any event is likely to be most variable, both because the higher esoteric includes our individual psychological response – the individual unconscious – and our understanding of the event according to our mental model of the world – our own personal version of the higher esoteric belief structure that our culture initiates us into. Both of these tie in with some of the most fundamental questions of consciousness and human nature.

If the hero's journey is the integration of a mostly unconscious response to an event of great importance (a sacred event) into consciousness, then we can say that the esoteric metamorphosis is this process of integration. But, almost by definition, what this means is that we do not understand the event until after it is over. While we are living through it, our perception is dominated by emotions, feelings, and mostly unconscious responses. Only truly sacred events trigger this kind of response because we are taken out of the normal, everyday world that we consciously understand and are thrust into a world that we do not understand. Understanding comes later. How much later it comes is a question to which there is no fixed answer. It may be hours, days, weeks, or even years. We may go a lifetime never being able to make sense of something that happened to us. In that case, a hero's journey has not taken place because the hero's journey requires the integration of the event into consciousness, and that integration takes place at the higher esoteric.

If we think back to Shakespeare's greatest tragedies, all of them feature a section at the end of the story where the tragic hero realises what they have done and comes to terms with the implications of it. In the case of King Lear, all of the second half of the story is about Lear's desperate attempt to make sense of what has happened. For the others, the period of realisation is shorter, but no less dramatic. Macbeth's lament is one of the most memorable: "*Out, out, brief candle!/Life's but a walking shadow, a poor player/That struts and frets his hour upon the stage/And then is heard no more.*" The final transcendence in all of these stories occurs at the higher esoteric, not just as a psychological event, but as an incorporation into consciousness. That is what the hero's journey is about in its highest manifestation.

Just as our own hero's journeys are about the personal journey we must make to integrate something that was previously unconscious into our own *higher esoteric*, the greatest stories in any culture reveal the deepest truths of that culture. They are initiatory to the extent that they make us feel those truths and perhaps eventually even understand them. In his own day, the works of Shakespeare were considered very poorly. The Bard only really became popular in the 19th century. Something had changed in Western culture that made the things communicated by Shakespeare resonate with the general culture. One of those things is the tragic view of life.

This brings us to the final point to make about the difference between rites of passage and hero's journeys. It is the genre of tragedy which makes that point in the clearest terms, because it is predicated on the "failure" of the hero. Romeo and Juliet, Hamlet and Ophelia, Othello and Desdemona, Macbeth and Lady Macbeth, King Lear and his daughters—all of them are socially ruined by their failure to navigate the exoteric metamorphosis they are confronted with in their respective stories. That is, before they die, their social identity is destroyed. (Note that this is the same thing that happens to Oedipus in Sophocles' great tragedies). Nevertheless, each of them completes a hero's journey. The completion of that hero's journey comes only when they accept their "failure" and come to terms with it. But this is not quite the right way to think about it. What they are coming to grips with is the sacrifice they have made. That sacrifice is of their socio-cultural identity; the same identity that is conferred by the rites of passage. The implication is that the highest version of the hero's journey can only ever be a subjective, esoteric experience. Tragedy represents this fact by having the hero lose everything but still transcend to the higher esoteric.

To say it again, the "failure" of the hero is really the sacrifice that they are making in order to transcend to the higher esoteric. Consider the case of King Lear. Lear begins his story as a powerful king with three beautiful daughters and ends it with nothing. He loses his social status, his wealth, his family, and basically all other aspects of his identity. In the words of his fool, he becomes *nothing*. From an external, exoteric, socio-cultural point of view, Lear is a failure. However, from an esoteric point of view, Lear has still gained something. He has made a sacrifice and received something for it on the other side of the process. What he has received is knowledge of the higher esoteric. The Lear we meet at the start of the play might be powerful and successful, but he is also vainglorious and tyrannical. He is lacking in virtue. His hero's journey is to learn what virtue means. Lear begins the story with everything the world can offer except virtue. He would not even know how to identify it, as evidenced by the fact that he ignores the wise counsel given to him at the beginning of the story. He must sacrifice all his worldly possessions and all his exoteric status to gain this esoteric knowledge.

We see the same arc in the trilogy of plays about Oedipus written by the ancient Greek tragedian Sophocles. The great king has all his power removed from him and ends up nothing more than a blind pauper. In *Oedipus at Colonus*, the old king is not only a blind pauper; he has been kicked out of his home and made to wander the countryside with only his faithful daughter, Antigone, as a companion. When we understand that ostracism (being expelled from your community) was considered a fate worse than death by the Greeks, we understand that Oedipus represents complete destitution. From an exoteric point of view, he is the lowest and the low. Yet Sophocles shows us that he is not broken because he still has his mind and integrity of character. Exoterically, he has nothing. Esoterically, he is still a king. The confrontation between Oedipus and Creon, which forms the centrepiece of the play, is a faceoff between the new and the old king. Creon has taken the throne that once belonged to Oedipus. He has inherited the socio-cultural position that Oedipus has lost. But Sophocles makes clear that Oedipus is the superior man. He is superior because he has connected with the higher esoteric, while Creon has not. It is for that reason that Oedipus' thundering denunciation of Creon is one of the greatest scenes ever written. Oedipus has sacrificed all his worldly goods for something greater.

The rites of passage can confer on us political power, economic wealth, or religious prestige. But they can never guarantee a connection to the higher esoteric. Creon is the leader of his society. He is a far more powerful man than Oedipus, but Oedipus is the superior man because he knows what virtue is from direct experience. For the same reason, the Lear we meet at the end of Shakespeare's great play is superior to the one we meet at the beginning, even though he is ruined. What the tragic hero's journeys show us is that "failure" is necessary to attain knowledge of the higher esoteric. All of Shakespeare's and Sophocles' tragic heroes are failures of this kind. But this is not actual failure; it is sacrifice. They have sacrificed all the other aspects of their identity: their health, their wealth, their power, and their families. Tragedy shows that access to the higher esoteric comes by sacrificing all the other aspects of life. Only the hero's journey can show us this form of initiation. That is why we say that the hero's journey is the metamorphosis into the higher esoteric, while the rites of passage are first and foremost socio-cultural metamorphoses.

The Cycle-Ending-in-Transcendence

At the start of this chapter, we said that we could use the rites of passage and hero's journeys to better understand the archetypes themselves. We have made a number of connections in this respect. Firstly, we noted that, although every culture has numerous rites and stories that are used on a regular basis as part of everyday life, the most important of those rites and stories are concerned with the archetypal metamorphosis periods. This is clearest in relation to rites of passage. It seems that every society marks birth, initiation, marriage, childbirth, and death with the most meaningful and elaborate rites and ceremonies. Because the hero's journey is concerned with the esoteric side of metamorphosis and specifically its higher esoteric aspects, there are no hero's journeys featuring babies or young children because at that age we are not capable of integrating events into consciousness. Thus, the major stories in any culture focus on heroes from late childhood onwards.

The second point we made is that one of the reasons for this focus on the archetypal metamorphoses is because rites and stories are initiatory. We know from our discussion earlier in the book that the metamorphosis period is the most difficult because it requires a reconfiguration of character across all dimensions of identity. We have identified a number of pathologies that can occur as a result of these difficulties. The rites and stories are there to mitigate the risk and assist us through the metamorphoses by showing us the journey that others have taken before us. In the case of rites, these are public ceremonies, and we learn by observation. By the time of our own marriage, for example, we would have certainly attended a number of marriage ceremonies as guests. Therefore, we have some level of knowledge about what is required when our turn comes. Stories, myths, and legends work in a similar fashion by presenting to our minds a compelling hero and going into detail about the challenges they face and the virtues they must call on to overcome them. Just like the major rites of passage map to the archetypal phases of life, so too do the major stories in every culture feature heroes going through the archetypal challenges. Thus, we have seen that Shakespeare gives us Orphan heroes in Romeo, Juliet, Hamlet, Ophelia, Bendick, Beatrice, Claudio, and Hero. He gives us Adult heroes in Othello, Desdemona, Macbeth, Lady Macbeth, and Richard III. Finally, he gives us the Elder hero of King Lear. If we were to do a review of the most important stories in any culture and any time in history, we would inevitably find that those stories involve the hero going through an archetypal metamorphosis.

In this way, the rites and the stories of our culture communicate in an overt fashion what to expect during the archetypal metamorphoses by showing what will be required of us at the time, including what clothes we will need to wear, what forms of address we must use, and even where we will need to stand and how to behave. All of these factors are specific to the culture in question. But what both van Gennep and Campbell realised was that, beneath this vast array of surface differences, what unified the rites and stories from across cultures was the underlying structure which we have identified as a cycle that has three segments. We have seen that a crucial feature of this cycle is that there must be something on the line; the hero of the story or the initiate of the rite of passage must make a sacrifice. That is why van Gennep said that the cycle is a journey into the sacred and a return to wholeness on the other side. That is also why the association of the cycle with the metamorphosis period of the archetypes is perfectly fitting because we sacrifice our old archetypal identity and accept the new one. That is a process that takes time. While we are going through that process, we are in sacred status, undergoing the sacrifice.

Thus, it turns out that the rites and stories of any culture communicate something at a deeper level. They may tell us about heroes, and they may show us initiates, and we may note down all the actions, the clothing, the ceremonial behaviour and everything else; all of that is valid, but what is sub-communicated is the underlying structure itself, the sacred cycle that contains three segments. We are almost never conscious of this cycle, which is why van Gennep and Campbell had to spend years uncovering it, but it gets transmitted to us subliminally every time we hear a story or witness a rite of passage. This is another reason why Campbell was correct to say that the hero's journey is a descent into the unconscious. Every story works its magic at a level deeper and more profound than consciousness.

Connecting the dots, we can see that the reason why rites and stories can initiate us into the archetypal metamorphosis is because the metamorphosis is also a cycle; a process featuring three distinct segments. This is exactly what we have already implied when we said that the metamorphosis requires us to sacrifice our old archetypal identity. Therefore, what is being communicated by the rites and stories is a subconscious understanding of the archetypal metamorphoses in general. We learn not just how to go through a specific metamorphosis as represented by a hero or initiate who manifests a specific archetype; we learn about the metamorphosis itself as a cycle. This is also the reason why the major stories and rites are synonymous with the religious practices of every culture, because they are invocations of the sacred.

To say it again, the archetypal metamorphosis period is the transition into sacred status. We must sacrifice one archetypal identity in order to gain the next. On the other side of the process, we have incorporated the new archetypal identity, and there begins the long period of what we have called stability, as we face the challenges and explore the opportunities of the new phase. We can never properly know what those challenges and opportunities are until we experience them. Thus, every metamorphosis and every archetypal phase must be a hero's journey into the unconscious and the unknown.

Since we find a shared pattern beneath the rites of passage, hero's journeys, and archetypes, it will assist us to abstract away from the specific details of each manifestation and name the structure directly. We know that the pattern is a cyclical process that involves a sacrifice. Now, it might be argued that this sacrifice represents a loss. For example, once we have left childhood, we may never go back. This is true in the biological sense that there is no way to return to a child's body once we have swapped it for that of an adult. Similarly, a reversion to childish mental states would be considered a psychological illness, and for society to treat an adult as if they were a child would be either a joke or some kind of abuse. The archetypal wheel turns only in one direction. We may never return to the earlier states.

The same is true for the rites of passage and the hero's journeys. A rite of passage is only meaningful if something is truly on the line. If this is not the case, any rite quickly devolves into little more than an empty ceremony. Similarly, any great story must feature a hero who has something to lose. The greatest of stories show us what that loss means to the hero and invite us to experience it for ourselves. What is on the line for King Lear is his legacy, including the welfare of his daughters. Hamlet's future and his right to the crown of Denmark are what are at stake in his story. For Macbeth and Othello, their marriages are at stake, not to mention their social status and prosperity. In addition to the personal consequences, all of these stories have significant political ramifications for the societies in which the heroes live.

For the archetypal metamorphosis, what is being sacrificed is the old archetypal identity. But this giving up of the old identity is not a negation of it. On the contrary, the latter is built upon the former. Our adult body does not come out of nowhere. It is predicated upon the child body that preceded it. We carry the physical scars of childhood into adulthood as evidence. Similarly, few would deny that at least some (maybe most) of our adult behaviour patterns are formulated in childhood. And our mature familial and socio-cultural identities are based on those we established in the Child and Orphan phases of life. The latter archetypal phases do not negate the earlier ones; they enhance and build on them.

The word which captures this fact is *transcendence.* Transcendence builds upon that which came before. Since the pattern that we have identified that unifies the rites of passage, hero's journey, and the archetypes is a cycle, and since each of these cycles involves a sacrifice that leads to transcendence, it follows that the unifying pattern we are looking for is the *cycle-ending-in-*

transcendence. The cycle-ending-in-transcendence is the process by which we incorporate something new into ourselves. That is why *incorporation* is the last of the three segments that van Gennep identified. A rite of passage incorporates something new in the socio-cultural sense. A hero's journey incorporates something new into consciousness. An archetypal phase of life incorporates a new character across the domains of identity.

The three segments of the cycle-ending-in-transcendence have a specific function and meaning. The separation phase causes a break with everyday life by creating the sacred space. In the case of rites of passage, this sacred space can be understood literally as a church or other holy building. But the sacred space must also be psychological or spiritual in nature. For the hero or initiate, this psychological sacred space comes from the sacrifice that they are required to make. If the sacrifice is not felt as such, then there is no journey into the sacred. Thus, the separation phase of the cycle establishes the sacrifice both in the socio-cultural sense where that is relevant and also psychologically and spiritually in the hero/initiate.

We have said that the transition phase of the cycle is the elaboration of the meaning of the sacrifice and also potentially a test of the hero/initiate. We can now think of it as the hero/initiate's response to the sacrifice required of them. In a rite of passage, it is the Elder's task to explain the meaning of the rite and to lay out the challenge for the initiate. Interestingly, what Campbell found was that most of the great mythical stories also contain an Elder archetype whose role is to guide the hero. In any case, the purpose of the transition phase of the cycle is to test that the initiate is capable of making the sacrifice required of them.

With the test passed, the incorporation phase then sanctifies and fulfils the sacrifice. This is the point of no return. The hero/initiate has one last chance to back out. To proceed is to sanctify the metamorphosis by a socio-cultural change of status, as in a rite of passage, a psycho-spiritual one as in a hero's journey, or a complete change of character, as in an archetypal transition. This is the transcendence part of the cycle.

Now that we have identified the general pattern, we may apply it back to any of the cycles we have seen in this book.

All of the stories we have looked at are cycles-ending-in-transcendence. Consider Luke Skywalker's journey in the original Star Wars trilogy. He begins as a naive farm boy in the outer reaches of the galaxy. The separation phase of the story is when his aunt and uncle are killed. He must sacrifice his life on the farm and step into the transition period of education and training given by his Elders, Obi-Wan and Yoda. The incorporation phase of the story sees him graduate into an Adult identity as a Jedi Knight. Alongside this esoteric metamorphosis, he has also incorporated a new social and political identity, new friends, and a new understanding of his place in his family.

All of the rites of passage we have looked at in this book are cycles-ending-in-transcendence. We can see that pregnancy and childbirth fit the pattern. At the biological level, conception is the separation phase of the cycle. The pregnancy itself is the transition phase. Labour and birth are the incorporation phase. What is incorporated (again, literally *in-corporated* in the biological sense) is a new human being. But that new person is also incorporated as a member of a family (biological-familial domain), a member of society (socio-cultural domain), and a new arrival of whatever the culture in question understands as a manifestation of the higher esoteric (a soul, a spirit, a child of God).

Most importantly, all of the archetypal metamorphoses we have analysed are cycles-ending-in-transcendence. The Child separates (literally) from the Mother and begins a rapid transition period where it must acclimatise to the environment in which it finds itself. The rapid growth of the body and the building of the immune system attune the Child to the world. The incorporation phase ends when the Child has attained the major biological faculties it needs to get through that phase of life.

The Orphan metamorphosis requires the separation from the Child's body (puberty), the Child's socio-cultural identity (family), and the Child's higher esoteric dependence on the parents. The transition phase requires the Orphan to come to grips with sexual maturity, the psychic birth of the ego, and the initiation into the socio-cultural institutions of society. Once these changes are incorporated, there begins the long period of training and education moving towards the mature Adult identity.

The Adult must separate from the freedom and possibility of the Orphan phase of life and accept the responsibilities of maturity. In the familial domain, this begins with marriage and the arrival of the first Child. In the socio-cultural domain, it begins with full membership in the economic, political, military, and religious institutions with the associated burden of now being a full and productive member. The higher esoteric transcendence is the acceptance of these responsibilities and the discipline to see them through over a period of decades.

The Elder's separation phase in the familial domain comes with the maturity and independence of their own children, who are now able to support themselves. With the separation from an intense period of responsibility and duty, the Elder is now able to confront the higher esoteric questions of value and purpose most directly. As Jung put it, this is the incorporation of the soul.

Note that the separation, transition, and incorporation pattern also applies to the archetypal pairs. Each archetypal phase involves the separation from the previous pair and the incorporation of the new. Even the Child must (physically) separate from the Mother before being incorporated into the family. The Orphan must separate from the Parents to incorporate the Elder. The Adult must separate from the Elder to incorporate their own Child. Finally, the Parents separate from their Child to become an Elder and incorporate the Orphan. These separations and incorporations resonate across the three levels of being, especially the socio-cultural and higher esoteric, where the rites of passage overtly signal the deprecation of the old pair and the formation of the new.

We need to emphasise here that, although this way of talking about the cycles-ending-in-transcendence makes sense within our analytical framework, life is not an accounting ledger. We do not consciously weigh up the gains against the costs and choose rationally. The offer of transcendence comes upon us not from a place of rationality but from the deep, dark depths of the unconscious. For this reason, the psychological experience of transcendence begins with a feeling of loss. This makes sense because the sacrifice comes at the beginning of the process. The separation phase asks us to accept the sacrifice, trusting that everything will work out in the long run.

This is why the concept of the sacred is so often conjoined with the notion of faith. To sacrifice without knowing whether you will get anything in return requires faith. To let go of something you know and understand for something you don't know and don't understand requires faith. Another reason why the the rites of passage and the hero's journeys are initiatory is because they instil in us faith in the process. They subcommunicate to us the cycle-ending-in-transcendence. They show us heroes who make a sacrifice and put everything on the line even though the stakes are high and the outcome is not guaranteed. Once again, tragedy proves itself to be the supreme art form because it gives us heroes who failed and yet still experienced an esoteric transcendence. Tragedy shows that even when we think we have lost everything, there is still a transcendence that may come to us.

Once we understand that the archetypes themselves are cycles-ending-in-transcendence, we can make sense of a fact we pointed out back in chapter two. Life is an ascent through the levels of being. The beginning of life takes place almost entirely at the biological level. We are physically entirely dependent on our parents during this time, and our sole need is the physical attention that they give us. The cycle-ending-in-transcendence during the Child archetypal phase is primarily biological in nature.

Through the Orphan and Adult phases of life, the socio-cultural becomes dominant. We must find our place in society in the economic, political, and religious sense. Society provides for us ready-made social scripts in the form of rites of passage and other ceremonies that guide us through this phase by inducting us into the institutions of society. Learning to navigate those institutions is our main task. The cycle-ending-in-transcendence during this time is primarily socio-cultural in nature.

Finally, we get to the Elder phase of life, where the higher esoteric dominates. What the stories of King Lear and Oedipus show us is that the higher esoteric exists beyond and above both the biological and socio-cultural. We may lose almost everything at the lower levels of beings, and still something remains left over. That something is the higher esoteric. The sacrifice of the lower levels leads to transcendence to the higher esoteric.

Mapped against our earlier diagram about the progression of the archetypes, we may capture the archetypal transcendence through the levels of being as follows:-

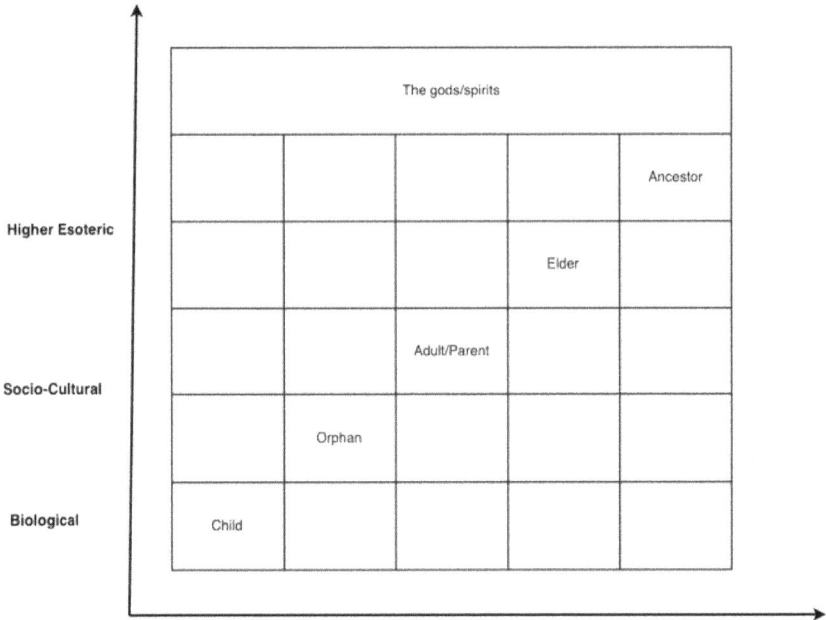

The boundaries between the archetypes are the metamorphosis periods. These are cycles-ending-in-transcendence that require us to sacrifice the previous archetype and step into the new. But the pattern we see more broadly from this diagram is that the archetypes themselves are also cycles-ending-in-transcendence. The ascent through the levels of being is not at the expense of the lower levels; rather, the resonance increases over the course of life to incorporate the biological, socio-cultural, and higher esoteric. That is why the hero's journey becomes more important in the second half of life; we are more able to understand and integrate events into consciousness, including deepening our understanding of our experiences from earlier in life. Yet another reason why we say that the hero's journey is primarily esoteric is because we can undergo a re-evaluation of an earlier experience entirely in a psychological or spiritual fashion. The great stories can assist us in this process by inviting us to compare our own experience against that of a cultural hero. Such a comparison can change our understanding of ourselves and the world in an entirely esoteric fashion. The cycle-ending-in-transcendence can then be said to take place entirely in the higher esoteric domain, but it would still follow the separation, transition, and incorporation pattern.

Conclusion

We said at the beginning of the book that the archetypes represent qualitatively different phases of life, implying a metamorphosis in identity that must take place between them. There are two main ways in which this chapter has added to our understanding of this dynamic.

Firstly, we have seen that both the rites of passage and the hero's journeys are initiatory devices whose purpose is to facilitate the metamorphosis between the archetypes. Built into the structure of these is the notion of sacrifice. We must give up one archetypal identity in order to create the next. But this giving up is not a renunciation but rather a transcendence. Thus, the qualitative differences between the archetypes come as we transcend the levels of being, beginning with the biological phase of childhood, the socio-cultural phase of adolescence and adulthood, and the higher esoteric phase of elderhood. What this means is that our own journey becomes more and more individual as we ascend to the higher esoteric.

The second key point of this chapter has been that the underlying pattern is the same for the rites of passage, the hero's journeys, and the archetypal phases. They are all cycles-ending-in-transcendence, requiring a sacrifice of the hero/initiate, and containing the three segments of separation, transition, and incorporation. But if what we said above is true and the major rites of passage and hero's journeys are the archetypal metamorphoses, then it follows that these are embedded in the archetypes themselves. Since the archetype is also a cycle-ending-in-transcendence, this means we have cycles embedded in cycles.

In mathematics, a pattern which repeats itself at different scales is called a fractal. The argument that we will make in the final chapter of this book is that the rites of passage and the hero's journeys are fractals of the archetypes. If that's true, then the archetypes may also be fractals of something at an even larger scale. There is a deeper unity at play which we will now explore.

Chapter 5: The Human Archetype

We started this book with a relatively small set of concepts. The archetypes are qualitatively different phases of life; the levels of being are the main dimensions of quality, while the exoteric-esoteric distinction denotes whether the quality is internal to the individual or faces outwards to the society to which the individual belongs. In the last chapter, we added the rites of passage and hero's journeys to the list and found that they follow the exact same pattern as the archetypes in that they resonate across the levels of being and have an exoteric-esoteric aspect. In fact, the rites of passage and the hero's journeys are just two sides of the same coin. More specifically, they are two sides of the same cycle, one referring to its exoteric, socio-cultural aspect (rites) and the other to its esoteric, inner aspect (hero's journey).

Having spent an entire book outlining the differences between these concepts, our challenge in this final chapter is to understand that there is no difference. All along, we have been talking about just one pattern; it is the cycle-ending-in-transcendence, which resonates across the levels of being and has an exoteric and an esoteric aspect. The archetypes, rites of passage, and hero's journeys are all cycles. The only difference between them is scale; the archetypes cycle over years, while the rites and hero's journeys normally take days or months.

It is because of this difference in scale that we can analyse the rites and hero's journeys as being contained within the archetypes. But that is merely a side effect of the crucial point that will motivate this final chapter of the book. Earlier, we associated the rites and hero's journeys with the metamorphosis that begins each archetypal phase. They are not just cycles that happen to be contained within the larger cycle; they are a crucial component of that larger cycle. What this means is that what we have been calling the archetypal metamorphosis is itself a cycle-ending-in-transcendence. We transcend from the metamorphosis into what we have been calling the stability phase of the archetype. That division has served us well until now. But what we will need to understand in this chapter is that the archetype itself has not two but three phases, the same phases as the rites and hero's journeys.

If that is true, then it means that the archetypes are a larger-scale cycle that has the exact same three-part structure as the smaller cycles of the rites and hero's journeys. Since the rites and hero's journeys are embedded within the archetype, we find a pattern that recurs at different scales. In mathematics, this is called a fractal. As we will see later in the chapter, there are at least six degrees of fractal relationships at play, meaning we can zoom in at least six times to find smaller and smaller cycles embedded within the larger ones. This is one way to understand the meaning of the fractal nature of the cycle-ending-in-transcendence.

But the mathematical concept misses what is the more important point about the embeddedness of the rites and hero's journeys, which is that the hierarchical relationship is what creates meaning and purpose. The meaning of the smaller cycles is governed by the larger ones. That is where the qualitative differences between the archetypes become relevant again. The abstract pattern may repeat itself, but it does so over a number of qualitative differences. The rites and hero's journeys that pertain to the Orphan archetype, for example, get their meaning and purpose from the qualities of that phase of life.

The English language provides us with a way to understand the nature of embedded meaning. In English, we can have clauses embedded in a sentence. When that happens, the meaning of the embedded clause is determined by the main clause. Take the following example:-

The thief, running out of ideas, picked up the gun.

The embedded clause here is *running out of ideas.* It gets its colour, its flavour, and its quality from the main clause, which is *The thief picked up the gun.* Bad things normally happen when thieves snatch at guns, so this example of *running out of ideas* is quite dramatic.

If we take the same clause and embed it in a different main clause, the meaning would change.

The writer, running out of ideas, threw down the pen.

This case of *running out of ideas* is far less dramatic, at least on the assumption that the frustrated writer doesn't also have a gun nearby. Although, even if he did, we presume he would be more of a danger to himself than others.

The point is that the same sequence of words, although its core meaning remains relatively stable, nevertheless gets much of its quality from the overarching structure in which it is embedded. The same goes for our cycles-ending-in-transcendence. The smaller cycles, the rites of passage and hero's journeys, are embedded in the larger cycles of the archetypes. The archetypes are like the main clauses of the sentence. They set the overall meaning. We know in detail what those meanings are because we have spent the majority of the book exploring them. Thus, our task in this chapter is to understand how the fractal cycle concept creates a hierarchy of embedded meaning that flows from the archetypes down.

A preliminary way to think about that is to take a recurring rite of passage and imagine how its meaning changes over the course of life. For example, Catholics go to Mass once a week. The underlying structure of Mass is always the same, even though the content changes somewhat from week to week. During the Child phase of life, we would expect the individual to understand very little about the meaning of Mass as a whole, or the individual segments of it. It is the during the Orphan phase of life when more active engagement is required, symbolised by the fact that the individual now receives the Eucharist. This understanding increases over the Adult and Elder phases where informal opportunities for more active teaching roles arise for long-time members of the congregation. In short, we would expect the understanding of Mass to reflect the archetypal phase the individual is in. For the Child, simply being physically present is all that can be expected. For Orphans and Adults, the socio-cultural aspects may predominate. For the Elder, the deeper meanings come to the fore. The Mass is always the same, but its meaning changes depending on the archetype in which it is embedded.

Although a hero's journey is not formally repeatable in the way that a rite of passage is, the same principle applies. Without knowing anything about the specific details, we can make some very accurate guesses about the nature of any hero's journey based on what archetypal phase it occurs in. This fact is reflected in the literary genres that demarcate the hero of the story based on age. Children's literature does not contain any advanced spiritual or intellectual revelations or difficult moral dilemmas because these simply aren't relevant to the Child archetype. Similarly, it would be strange for a hero's journey featuring an Elder to include nervousness and anxiety caused by peer pressure, since that scenario is more fitting for the Orphan.

These relationships between the archetypes and the rites of passage and hero's journeys are fairly straightforward, but, as has been the case throughout the book, what seems simple at first glance turns out to be more complex on closer investigation. The cycle-ending-in-transcendence resonates across the three levels of being and has an exoteric and an esoteric aspect. But now we see that the cycle is itself made up of nested cycles, each of which requires a transcendence and each of which also resonates across the qualitative categories we have used throughout the book. Furthermore, since our own individual cycle-ending-in-transcendence is part of the collective cycle of our society, it can resonate "upwards" or "outwards" and change the frequency of the entire culture. We will shortly see an example of just that, where an isolated event in a forest in northern Germany triggered a monumental change in Western history.

To better understand the interactions of the fractal cycles-ending-in-transcendence, we will use what's called a tree diagram, which comes from computer programming, where it is used to demonstrate the concept known as *tree recursion*. The tree diagram is useful because we know that our cycle-ending-in-transcendence is comprised of three segments, which we have termed *separation*, *transition*, and *incorporation*. What we now need to grasp is that each of these individual segments is itself a cycle-ending-in-transcendence that has the same three-part structure. That means we can *drill down* into the segments and find another three-part cycle.

However, because of the fractal relationship at play, we know that any cycle must also be a component of a larger cycle. To find that, we need to *zoom out.* In short, beginning from any cycle-ending-in-transcendence, whether it be a rite of passage, a hero's journey, or an archetype, we expect to be able to *drill down* to lower-level cycles or *zoom out* to larger ones, just as we can start from a sentence and drill down to examine the embedded clauses or zoom out to examine the paragraph in which the sentence belongs. What we end up with is a hierarchy of relationships that create meaning.

Let's now work through some examples to demonstrate the concept.

Descending the Fractal Tree

We'll begin by showing an example of *drilling down* to the cycles at the lower levels, using the Catholic rite of Mass to demonstrate. We know that the Mass will have three segments: separation, transition, and incorporation. We can show that on our tree diagram as follows:-

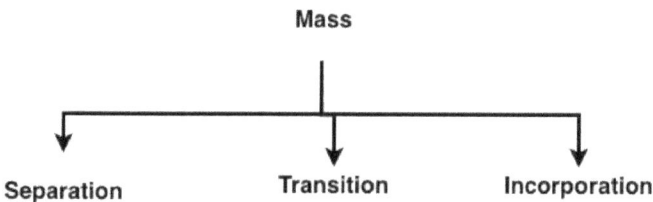

The separation phase of the Mass is the entry to the church itself. To step into church is to enter a sacred space that is distinct from everyday life. Most churches, especially Catholic ones, are designed to encourage the feeling of separation by creating an environment unlike anything that exists elsewhere. The entry of the congregation and priest and the introductory rites of the mass constitute the separation phase of the rite.

The transition phase is the main body of the service. In Catholic terminology, this is known as the Liturgy of the Word, which centres around three readings from the Bible.

Finally, there is the Liturgy of the Eucharist, which constitutes the incorporation phase. In the case of Catholic Mass, the meaning of *incorporation* is very precise. The Eucharist ritual is about incorporating the body of Christ in either literal or symbolic form depending on the flavour of the faith you follow.

We can now represent these specific details on our diagram, giving us the three-part breakdown of the cycle-ending-in-transcendence called Mass:-

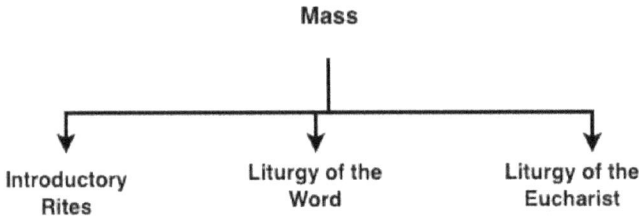

Mass

Introductory Rites   Liturgy of the Word   Liturgy of the Eucharist

Thinking back to our idea of embedded meaning, the top level of the tree is like the main clause in a sentence whose meaning governs the lower levels. This raises the question, "What is the meaning of Mass"? No doubt there are many different perspectives on that, but it should be uncontroversial to say that Mass is about receiving spiritual nourishment. This is symbolised during the incorporation phase of the rite (the Eucharist) via the receipt of bread and wine that represents the body of Christ, whose meaning comes from the Bible passage, "whoever feeds on my flesh and drinks my blood has eternal life." (John 6:54).

If the receipt of spiritual nourishment is the overall meaning, the three lower level cycles serve that purpose. It is clear that the Eucharist does, but so too does the Liturgy of the Word, which provides *nourishment* in the form of readings from the Bible. The Introductory Rites provide their nourishment in the form of homily, prayer, and personal reflection. Each of the three segments expands and enhances the overall meaning of the Mass.

This way of thinking about the rites of passage accords with our analysis earlier in the book. What we now need to understand is that the lower levels of the rite are themselves three-part cycles-ending-in-transcendence. This creates a second layer in the hierarchy of meaning. To return to our language analogy, it's like having an embedded clause within an embedded clause:-

The thief, running out of ideas, as he always did, picked up the gun.

This sentence is a little clumsy, but the meaning should be clear. The embedded clause *running out of ideas* now has its own embedded clause, *as he always did.* The meaning of this embedded clause modifies and expands on the one above it in the hierarchy of meaning. Of course, it also modifies the meaning of the overall sentence through the subordinate clause. We don't know whether the thief is always grabbing at his gun, but we can be pretty sure that his crimes are always haphazard affairs.

The exact same dynamic holds when we add a second layer of cycles-ending-in-transcendence to our model, although the amount of semantic complexity added thereby very much exceeds the linguistic example. Each top-level segment becomes itself a three-part cycle. In diagram form, it looks like this:-

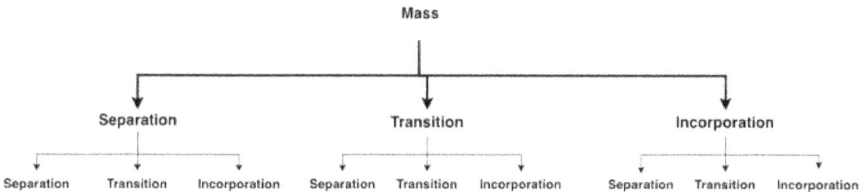

Remember that each of these is a cycle-ending-in-transcendence meaning that the completion of the lower level transcends upwards to sanctify and fulfil the node immediately above. Thus, the completion of the separation, transition, and incorporation phases for the top level Separation node represents the transcendence of that node, at which point the overall cycle moves on to the top-level Transition. But it's also true that the meaning of the lower-level nodes serves the node immediately above them in the same way that we just saw that the double embedded clause modifies the meaning of the embedded clause. This gets us into some difficult semantic terrain, so let's take a deep breath and once again use a real-world example to explain the abstract concepts.

We'll use just the separation phase of the Mass (Introductory Rites) to demonstrate. We expect this segment to have our familiar three-part structure as follows:-

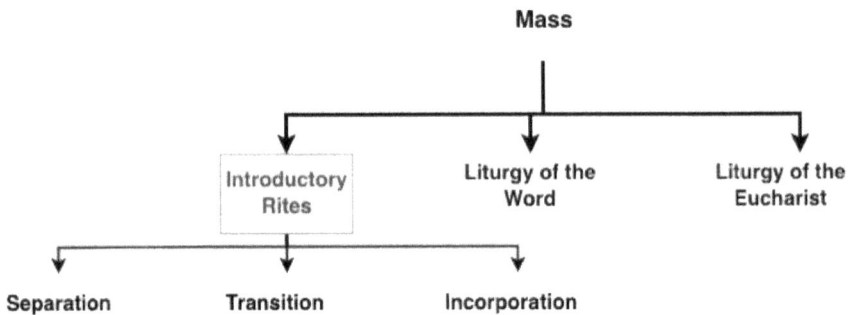

Mass

Introductory Rites | Liturgy of the Word | Liturgy of the Eucharist

Separation | Transition | Incorporation

The general meaning of these lower-level segments stays the same. The separation phase creates the sacred space by putting forward a sacrifice; the transition phase elaborates on it, and the incorporation phase sanctifies and fulfils it. But now, these three segments are modifying another Separation phase. That means that there is a separation phase of the Separation phase, i.e., there is a phase whose purpose is to create the sacred space for a higher-level phase that creates the sacred space for the overall rite. This sounds mind-bending, yet it is rather straightforward to understand how it works in reality.

The Introductory Rites of Mass are about creating the sacred space in which the redemption of sin and the receipt of spiritual nourishment can take place. The three nodes beneath it need to serve that purpose. In order for the Introductory Rites to achieve their purpose, we need the participants to physically gather in the sacred space and to mentally and spiritually prepare for the rite that follows. Specifically in relation to Mass, we need the congregation inside the church and primed for the receipt of the spiritual nourishment that comes later. This intermediate goal is sanctified and fulfilled when these requirements have been achieved. The achievement of these requirements is done via a three-part cycle-ending-in-transcendence.

Thus, the separation phase of the Introductory Rites is about physical entry to the church. The congregation arrives and enters. The priest and his entourage make their way to the altar, which the priest will kiss. The altar is a symbol of Christ and also of sacrifice more generally. The priest then greets the congregation and makes the sign of the cross. These actions create the sacred space at this lower level. With the purpose of the separation phase complete, we move to the transition phase.

The transition phase is supposed to elaborate on the sacrifice and to test the initiates. In the Introductory Rites, this is fulfilled by the Penitential Act, which asks all members of the congregation to reflect on their own sin. The test is to acknowledge sin and ask God for forgiveness. The more general creation of the sacred space in the separation phase is now enhanced and made personal for each initiate. This fulfils the transition phase, and we transcend to the incorporation phase.

The purpose of the incorporation phase is to sanctify and fulfil the sacrifice created by the first two phases. Now, we must remember here that, in terms of the overall Mass, we are still in the Separation phase at the higher level. The receipt of spiritual nourishment and the redemption of sin do not come until later in the rite. Therefore, we don't expect the incorporation phase at this lower level to achieve the goals of the overall Mass; rather, it needs to achieve the intermediate goal of Separation. It does this via the Collect Prayer, which the priest tailors to the specific meaning of this particular Mass. The theme explored in the Collect Prayer will become the theme of the spiritual nourishment of the overall Mass. Therefore, the Collect Prayer sanctifies and fulfils the meaning of the Separation phase itself, which is to create the sacred space in which spiritual nourishment will be received. With the segments of the lower-level cycle fulfilled, the Separation phase of the overall Mass is now sanctified. The congregation is physically and spiritually in the sacred space and ready to receive the main body of the rite. The Mass then transcends to the Incorporation phase (Liturgy of the Word) of the overall rite.

Adding all this to our diagram looks as follows:-

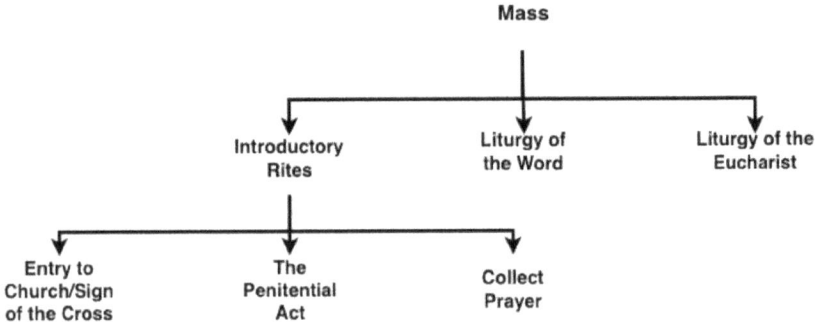

As if all that wasn't enough, we can go down one more level to find even more cycles-ending-in-transcendence. We just analysed the lower level separation phase as the entry to the church. But we can zoom in further and note that entry to the church first requires travel to the church. This is also a three-part cycle-ending-in-transcendence. We can add it to the tree diagram as follows:-

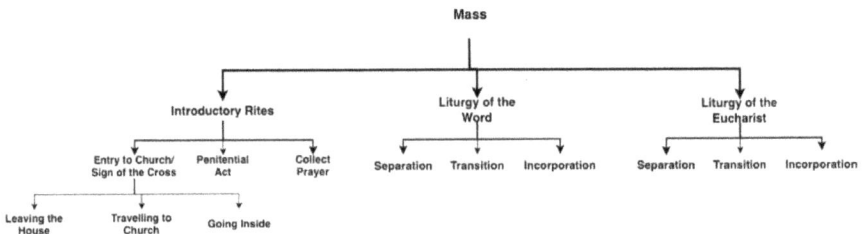

This analysis may seem unbearably trivial. And, in the way it is written, it certainly is. It is a tautology to say that in order to get to church, you must first travel there. However, recall that earlier in the book we found that a tautology at the physical and biological levels of being may not be a tautology at the higher levels. In fact, there is something very profound hidden away here.

What we have represented above is the separation phase of a separation phase. Remember what the purpose of the separation phase is: it causes a break with the everyday world by creating a sacrifice. At first glance, there is nothing about travelling to church that seems sacrificial. Yet that is not true. What the initiate is sacrificing is the possibility to do any other thing during that time. Just like marriage sacrifices the option to marry any other person, attending Mass sacrifices the option to do any other activity. Going to Mass, or any other rite of passage, requires us to create a space in our lives. Before we even begin the physical journey, we have held a space open in our mind, and maybe even our heart. That space holds the intention to attend Mass. That space is sacred because it implies a sacrifice, but that sacrifice exists in the esoteric realm only. This is not a trivial fact. It is in some ways the most important of facts. This sacred space of intent and will testifies to our beliefs at the higher esoteric level of being. We are always sacrificing to our conception of the higher esoteric. It is almost the definition of the higher esoteric that it constitutes whatever we makes sacrifices for.

What this crucial truth reveals is that our analysis until this point has had an inherently exoteric bias to it. We have focused on the external activities that people go through. They travel to church, they enter the building, they take part of the Penitential Act, and so on. We picture them as if we are watching an actor in a movie. But the reason we have called the top level of being the *higher esoteric* is because the esoteric really is the most important thing. What precedes the physical actions to take part in the rite of Mass is intention and will. These are esoteric in nature. What's more, the sacrifice in any rite of passage is primarily an esoteric one. If we don't feel it esoterically, there is no sacrifice and any rite becomes an empty ceremony of going through the motions.

If we return back to the tree diagram above, we now understand that the sacrifice made at the lowest level in the chain resonates upwards. The concept of transcendence creates a hierarchy of meanings which *stack up* to higher levels of being. The real *separation* phase of Mass begins with the intention to go to Mass and the creation of a (sacred) space in one's life. That leads to physical *separation* from everyday life as you leave your house and travel to the sacred space. Once you are in the sacred space physically, there is a spiritual *separation* brought about by the Introductory Rites. From a seemingly minor *separation*, which is the intent to travel to church, we transcend all the way up to a *separation* that encompasses the higher esoteric beliefs of Catholic theology. Within that theology, what is at stake is nothing more or less than the redemption of sin.

Our act of descending the fractal tree is kind of like focusing in with a camera. We see things at a higher level of resolution. But the tree also enables us to zoom out again and see the connections between all the elements. Small actions like getting your car keys, locking the door to the house, and beginning the journey to church no longer exist in isolation but in relation to the entire rite of passage and, indeed, the entire life of the person who is not just randomly going to church for the fun of it but because they hold the Catholic beliefs as their model of the higher esoteric level of being. We'll talk about this more in the next section when we focus on ascending the fractal tree.

Our drilling down exercise in this section has focused mostly on what can be observed externally about a rite of passage. This is not in itself a bad thing, as long as we keep in mind that there is also an esoteric side of the coin. Focusing on the exoteric raises some very old philosophical questions. How deep does the fractal pattern go? Is there a base level at which the fractal breaks down into component parts? Are these component parts, like atoms, the core elements that we can use to rebuild the cycle from scratch?

In our case, these questions do not really work since we have already identified the core pattern as the cycle-ending-in-transcendence, and this cannot be further analysed because to break the cycle is to render it into something qualitatively different. Similarly, because the concept of transcendence is built-in to the pattern, any lower-level cycle that does not connect to a higher one via transcendence is also something different. These disconnected elements may still have some meaning, in the way that a single sentence can have meaning, but that meaning does not connect with anything larger and therefore has no transcendence by definition.

There is a more pragmatic issue in relation to drilling down into the fractal cycles, and that is the fact that, even if there were an infinite number of lower-level cycles, we could not perceive them. We have to remember that just like language is the creation of finite beings, so too are rites of passage. There are limitations that come with being human. In theory, there can be an infinite number of embedded clauses in a single sentence. In practice, such a sentence would not be understandable by us mere mortals. The limits on the length and complexity of the sentence are not due to the structure of language but to the limitations of human memory and cognition. The same is true with the rites of passage. It would be theoretically possible to have a rite of passage with many lower levels that are all cycles-ending-in-transcendence, but such a rite could never be executed without training, rehearsals, and a great deal of organisation. At some level of complexity, there would not be enough time to both train for and then perform the rite correctly.

These limitations are no doubt one reason why the number of lower levels in a rite of passage is finite. A second, more important reason is that most religions and theologies have not been primarily concerned with the lower levels but with the higher ones. It is the higher levels that determine the meanings of the lower, and religion has typically sought after the highest levels of meaning. To perceive those requires not a *drilling down* but a *zooming out*. Having shown what it means to explore the fractal cycle-ending-in-transcendence by drilling down, let's now go through an example of zooming out, or ascending the tree.

Ascending the Fractal Tree

Now that we are familiar with how the hierarchy of embedded meanings that is created by nested cycles works, our task in this section is quite simple, since all we will be doing is pointing out that the rites of passage get their meaning from the higher-level cycles of the archetypes. We have already provided the justification for this earlier in the book by noting that van Gennep's extensive cross-cultural research had shown that the major rites of passage in any society congregate around the archetypal metamorphoses of birth, initiation, marriage, pregnancy, and death. This is easily translatable into our now-familiar cycle-ending-in-transcendence pattern, since what we have been calling the metamorphosis is nothing more or less than the separation phase of the cycle which ushers in the new archetype.

But if the archetypes are indeed fractals of the rites of passage, we would expect them to have the same three-part structure, and so far we have only defined two: the metamorphosis and stability periods. This distinction has served us well, but we now need to be more precise about it.

The reason why the concept of archetypal metamorphosis works is that, unlike the rites of passage, which are created by humans to have fixed beginnings and endings, the archetypes are part of life, and life is a continuous flow. Therefore, the boundaries between the archetypes and their segments are less clean-cut. What we have been calling the metamorphosis period is, in fact, the combination of the incorporation phase of the last archetype and the separation phase of the next. We said earlier in the book that the metamorphosis period is as much about letting go of the last archetype as embracing the new, and we noted a set of pathologies that arise if the individual cannot relinquish their previous identity. Technically speaking, the *letting-go* process belongs to the incorporation phase of the cycle. There is a curious correspondence here with the Catholic Mass, since the word "mass" comes from the Latin *missa*, which meant to *let go* or *send off*. That is what the incorporation phase of the cycle is all about. Just as rites of passage require a *letting go*, so too do the archetypes.

In real life, we experience the separation and incorporation phases together. The reason is that, to paraphrase a Phil Collins lyric, *we don't know what we've got till we lose it*. First we lose our archetypal identity, and then we must let go of it. This brings us back to the concept of sacrifice, but now with a new twist. Sacrifice implies loss, and loss implies grief. There is a grieving process for our old archetypal identity, which has, in a metaphorical sense, *died*. We must let go of it, send it away. That is what the incorporation phase requires of us. However, it is only when we arrive at the separation phase of the next archetype that we have properly lost the old one. Therefore, the grieving process of letting go tends to occur during the separation phase. We were correct earlier to say that the metamorphosis includes both the letting go of the old and the acceptance of the new. In practice, these occur simultaneously.

Within our new way of thinking about it, we can see that the journey from one archetype to the next is a transcendence. The failure to let go of the last archetype is the failure to transcend. The individual is partly stuck in the last archetype. This can be true even in a biological sense, since most biological processes take place over time. But it is especially true in the socio-cultural and in the higher esoteric (psychological) domains. We saw a prime example earlier in the book of what happens when the socio-cultural transcendence does not happen when we analysed modern feminism. Meanwhile, the Devouring Mother or Peter Pan complexes highlight a problem at the higher esoteric (psychological) level of being. In any case, full transcendence must occur at the biological, socio-cultural, and higher esoteric levels of being.

If the incorporation phase is about letting go of the old, the separation phase is about accepting the challenge of the new. The separation phase of each archetype is therefore directly analogous to the separation phase of Mass. It is complete when we are fully separated from the prior archetype at all three levels of being and ready to accept the challenges that the new archetype has for us. The rites of passage form an important part of that process since they are the socio-cultural event that confers the new archetypal identity by signalling to the wider society that the individual has made the transition.

Finally, we have the transition phase of the archetype which is what we have been calling the long stable period. This is synonymous with the attributes we associate with the archetypes more generally. It is the endless play of childhood, the *sturm und drang* of adolescence, the trials and tribulations of parenthood, and the stern but caring period of elderhood. Just as the transition phase of the rite of passage begins once the participants are fully separated from the everyday world and are ready to receive the rite, the transition period for an archetype begins when we have fully mourned the loss of the old archetypal identity and fully accepted the new. We are ready to face the new challenges that have been thrust upon us. The transition phase can be thought of as a test of character.

We can see, then, that the archetypes also fit within the three-part structure we have identified for the cycle-ending-in-transcendence:-

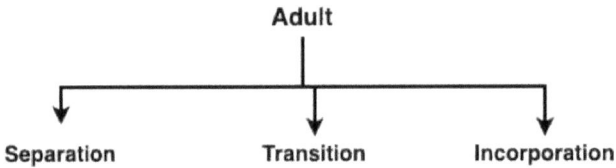

```
                        Adult
                          |
                          |
        ┌─────────────────┼─────────────────┐
        ↓                 ↓                 ↓
   Separation         Transition       Incorporation
```

Now that we have demonstrated that the archetypes fit the fractal pattern, it is a straightforward matter to connect any rite of passage with the larger cycle to which it belongs. Let's walk through an example to show how it works. Sticking within the Catholic tradition, we'll use the rite of Confirmation to demonstrate.

Rather than work through the details one step at a time, let's just present our diagram of Confirmation that includes the top-level separation, transition, and incorporation phases as well as the lower-level separation phase. This is the same analysis we just carried out for Mass. It looks as follows:-

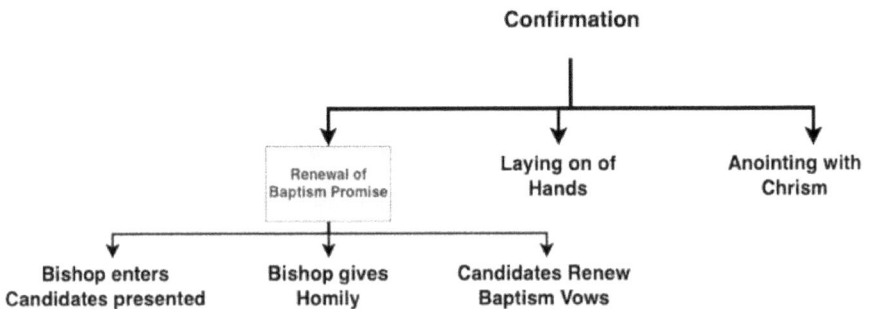

```
                                    Confirmation
                                         |
                                         |
            ┌────────────────────────────┼───────────────────────────┐
            ↓                            ↓                            ↓
      Renewal of                   Laying on of                 Anointing with
    Baptism Promise                    Hands                        Chrism
            |
   ┌────────┼────────────────┐
   ↓        ↓                ↓
Bishop enters   Bishop gives   Candidates Renew
Candidates presented  Homily    Baptism Vows
```

We need to briefly note a historical change that has occurred in relation to this rite. Confirmation is the third and final sacrament of Catholic initiation, which was originally a three-part ceremony that had Baptism, Communion, and Confirmation segments. In other words, Confirmation was originally the incorporation phase of a rite of passage that belonged to the Child phase of life. This changed over time so that, in the modern world, Confirmation is given at the onset of what we have called the Orphan phase.

If we think back to our analysis of the Orphan, what elements would we expect from a rite of passage that initiated this archetype? Remember that the main theme of the Orphan phase is the separation from the parents (Child-Parent pair) and the formation of the Orphan-Elder pair. There are several ways in which the Catholic rite of Confirmation affirms these. Firstly, Confirmation entails the formation of an Orphan-Elder relationship between the initiate and an older member of the congregation, who is given the task of preparing the initiate for the ceremony, but who also serves as a guide for many years afterwards. In addition, Confirmation is usually conducted not by a priest but by the higher-ranking Elder of bishop. Both of these can be seen as new Orphan-Elder relationships that are created.

We know from our earlier analysis that the creation of an Orphan-Elder relationship implies a deprecation in the Child-Parent one. Another way to think about it is that the Child must *separate* (there's that word again) from the parents. Confirmation carries out this separation by having the godparents of the initiate give them away (this could also be understood as the *letting go* of the incorporation phase of the Child) in the separation segment of Confirmation. This explicit deprecation of the Child-Parent relationship is reinforced by the fact that the separation phase also includes a reaffirmation of the baptism vows that were originally made by the godparents while the initiate was a Child. The initiate now reaffirms those vows, implying that they are deemed mature enough to make vows of their own will (Orphans have the ability to create their own sacred intents). Thus, the rite of Confirmation deprecates the Child-Parent (godparent) relationship in favour of the Orphan-Elder, exactly what is required for the separation phase of the Orphan archetype.

At the socio-cultural level, Confirmation signals the beginning of the religious identity associated with the Orphan phase of life. It confers a new status on the initiate within the congregation, who moves into a period of education and training for which they have been paired with a specific Elder from amongst the congregation. They will have new duties and responsibilities that go with this change of status.

Finally, there is the higher esoteric level of being. We already know that Confirmation corresponds to the metamorphosis we have called the psychic birth of the ego. Within the Catholic theology, that translates to the initiate receiving the Holy Spirit. In fact, it is the primary purpose of Confirmation to instil the Holy Spirit in the initiates. This purpose is sanctified during the third phase of the rite where the bishop anoints the initiates with chrism, making the sign of the cross on their forehead and saying, "Be sealed with the gift of the Holy Spirit". We can see that this "be sealed" is directly analogous to being made holy (whole), which is the purpose of the incorporation phase of the rite that sanctifies and fulfils the initiate with the Holy Spirit.

For all these reasons, we can see that Confirmation clearly belongs to the separation phase of the Orphan archetype and we can diagram this fact as follows:-

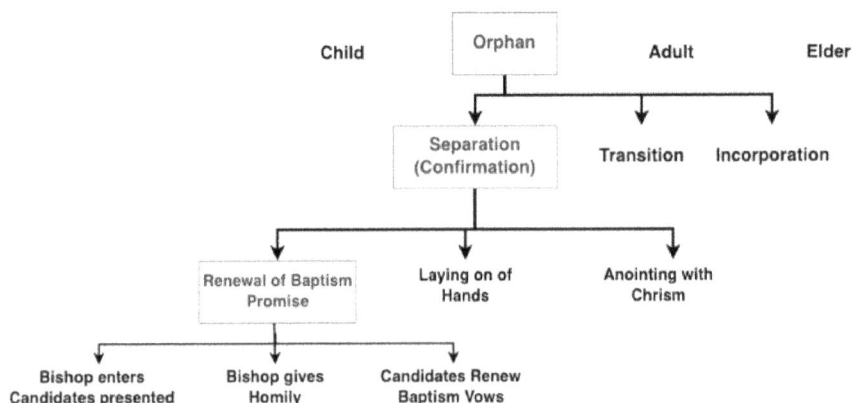

It is worth reiterating at this point that, although we have focused on Catholic rites, because the readership of this book is likely to have some familiarity with them, we expect to be able to perform this exact analysis on the corresponding rites from any culture. For example, we noted earlier in the book that the

Australian Aboriginal initiation for boys began with the physical removal of the initiate from the arms of his mother. Thus, the separation phase of that rite involves an explicit physical separation from the Parent. Although the content of that initiation is very different from Catholic Confirmation, we can see that both deprecate the status of the Parent and create the Orphan-Elder relationship. Moreover, both will follow the same fractal cycle pattern we have drawn above. The lower-level cycles connect upwards to the highest cycle in our schema, which is the archetype itself. This proves the point we set out to make in this section that we can ascend from the rites of passage upwards to the archetypes. Whether in a Catholic country, a hunter-gatherer tribe, or some other culture, it is the archetypal phase which determines the meaning of the rite of passage that marks its socio-cultural initiation.

Having demonstrated the nature of hierarchical meaning by both descending and ascending our fractal tree, we are now ready to return to the point we raised earlier on the exoteric bias of the rites of passage. Even in our analysis of Confirmation above, we yet again focused on the actions that are carried out during the rite because these are objective and verifiable, and their meaning is also amenable to symbolic interpretation. All of this is valid, but what it leaves out is how the initiate experiences the ceremony esoterically. When the bishop anoints their forehead with chrism, does the initiate actually feel that they have received the Holy Spirit? If not, then has the rite been successfully completed?

This is the same problem we talked of earlier in relation to the archetypes. We may have biologically and socio-culturally transitioned from the old archetype, but if we have not done so at the higher esoteric level, then full transcendence has not yet occurred, and we may expect a variety of psychological difficulties to follow. A rite of passage creates socio-cultural transcendence through the execution of physical actions. If you get through all the actions required of you during the Confirmation ceremony, then you have transcended as far as the socio-cultural level of being is concerned. But that doesn't mean you have transcended at the higher esoteric. Since a rite of passage can never guarantee transcendence at the higher esoteric level of being, we need the hero's journey concept to bridge the gap.

Fortunately, our new mode of analysis works just as well for the hero's journeys since they are also three-part cycles-ending-in-transcendence. Let's now show how our model can account for esoteric transcendence. We will once again use the life of Martin Luther as our subject matter.

Luther's Esoteric Transcendence

In our earlier analysis of the life of Luther, we went into some detail about his problematic attempt to become a monk due to his belief that the church had lost its esoteric purpose. There is a very specific event in Luther's life that led him to that conclusion, and it serves perfectly to further illustrate the difference between the rites of passage and the hero's journeys. But the story of Luther is especially poignant for our archetypology framework because the dramatic event that led him to join the monastery in the first place occurred when he already had an established archetypal identity. Luther was a twenty-one-year-old student at university coming to the end of a law degree. This places him in the latter part of the Orphan phase of life, not far away from graduating into adulthood as a professional lawyer.

In order to attain his identity as a student, we know that Luther must have gone through the rites of passage governing entry into university. As a Christian of his era, he would also have gone through the Catholic Church's rites, such as Confirmation. These are important facts because, even though he achieved the exoteric transcendence conferred by the rites, Luther had clearly not experienced any kind of corresponding esoteric transcendence. In fact, it's clear that he was not at all happy with the institutions he had been initiated into, as can be seen by his description of his *alma mater* as a "whorehouse and beerhouse". What's more, the idea of becoming a lawyer was not his own but one that his parents had foisted on him. We know from our earlier analysis that this is indicative of a dominant Child-Parent relationship, not an Orphan-Elder one. In short, although Luther had transcended at the biological and socio-cultural levels of being, he had not done so at the higher esoteric. His exoteric identity was established, but it lacked esoteric substance.

We can summarise the situation on our tree diagram as follows by noting that Luther was coming towards the end of the Orphan phase of life. But this was true only in the exoteric sense. Esoterically, something very different was going on, something that would lead to the dramatic event which would overturn Luther's exoteric identity and his whole life:-

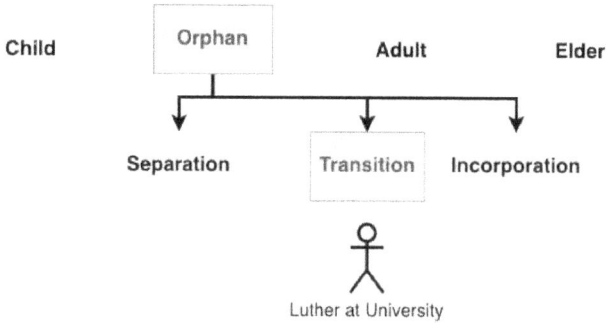

Luther at University

Luther was on the verge of graduating into an exoteric Adult identity that he had not chosen and was not happy with. That alone would not have made him unique. Like most young people in the same situation, he probably would have just gritted his teeth and gone on to become a lawyer. But that all changed after a dramatic episode that seemed to come out of nowhere.

Luther had been visiting his parents. While riding his horse back to the university, he found himself in a dense part of a forest when a violent thunderstorm blew over. A bolt of lightning struck nearby and threw him to the ground. Convinced he was about to die, Luther prayed to St. Anne to save him and, in return, promised to become a monk. When he survived the storm, he put his promise into action. He withdrew from university immediately. Two weeks later, he was enrolled in a monastery.

Even for the relatively religious age in which Luther lived, to throw away one's socio-cultural identity for what he claimed was divine intervention was not something that other people could understand. Luther's parents were furious, and his friends were perplexed. In the modern world, Luther would no doubt have been diagnosed as having a mental breakdown. But his story makes perfect sense within our archetypal framework.

Luther's life was devoid of meaning and independence (which often amounts to the same thing). He may have been coming to the end of the Orphan archetype, but he was still having his parents make decisions for him. This implies the absence of a meaningful Orphan-Elder relationship. Luther had gone through the exoteric motions of the Orphan archetype but had not engaged meaningfully with what should be the major character development of that archetype. The rites of passage that he had been through had not provided him any esoteric transcendence.

Whatever we think of the veracity of the divine intervention part of his near death episode, the result of that experience was to give Luther the esoteric transcendence he so desperately needed. His desire to join the monastery was sanctioned not by his parents but by his own conception of the higher esoteric (St. Anne). What's more, by joining the monastery, Luther would have the chance to form a new Orphan-Elder relationship. And that's exactly what happened. He was taken under the guidance of Johann von Staupitz, who became a key influence on his life.

Thus, what the esoteric transcendence of the near death experience did was to initiate Luther into a real Orphan dynamic. The problem was that, from all external appearances, Luther was already in the Orphan phase of life. In fact, he was coming to the end of it. That's why Luther's actions would have looked crazy and irrational to those close to him. But they were judging purely on exoteric criteria. Every cycle-ending-in-transcendence requires a sacred space to be opened up. That's what the near death experience did for Luther. He was no longer mindlessly following social scripts handed to him but forging his own way. Even at this early stage, we can see the courage that would become a defining feature of Luther's character: the courage to defy social expectations.

It's worth reiterating here that Luther would have gone through the Catholic rite of Confirmation earlier in his life. That rite of passage is supposed to create esoteric transcendence by instilling the initiate with the Holy Spirit. But we can see that this did not work for Luther; rather, it was the near-death experience in the forest which facilitated his transcendence. There are two key points about that. Firstly, the near death experience was a completely personal one. Nobody else was around at the time. Therefore, it had no socio-cultural aspect to it. That's why other people could not understand when Luther explained to them what had happened.

But perhaps the more interesting thing to note about the near-death experience is that it could never have been planned in advance, and yet it fell perfectly into our three-part cycle-ending-in-transcendence structure. Rites of passage can always be critiqued as being human contrivances. But what happened to Luther seemed to be a random act of nature. How can it be that an act of nature creates a cycle-ending-in-transcendence?

We'll return to that question shortly. For now, we need simply note that because what happened to Luther was a personal experience that had primarily esoteric meaning, we must analyse it as a hero's journey. Since we know that the hero's journey has the same three-part cyclical structure as the rite of passage, we can diagram Luther's experience in the forest in the exact same way we did earlier for the rite of Confirmation:-

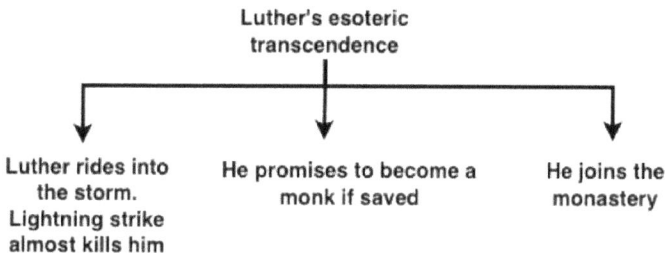

Remembering again the meaning of our three segments of separation, transition, and incorporation. We know that the separation phase must cause a break from the everyday world by creating a sacrifice. The transition phase is the explication of that sacrifice, the exploration of its full meaning, usually including a test of some kind for the initiate. Having passed the test, the incorporation phase completes the cycle by sanctifying the sacrifice, thereby making the initiate holy (whole) again. We can see that Luther's near-death experience is a perfect cycle-ending-in-transcendence.

The separation phase is the storm and the lightning bolt that throws Luther from his horse. This was no longer just a normal, everyday horse ride; it was a matter of life and death. The transition phase is Luther's response to being confronted with the possibility of death, which was to ask for divine intervention. Note that the request he made included a promise to join a monastery if saved. Luther proposed to sacrifice his existing exoteric identity to live a life dedicated to the esoteric. The incorporation phase sanctified that promise by saving Luther's life and setting him on a course to become a monk. He was made holy (whole) to the extent that his actions in joining the monastery brought his esoteric identity into alignment with his exoteric one. The final stage of the hero's journey *incorporated* his whole being.

These facts show that the lightning strike was a true cycle-ending-in-transcendence. But we already know that there was a larger transcendence at stake. Luther was going through the separation phase of the Orphan archetype at the higher esoteric level of being. Since he was doing so as a twenty-one-year-old, we say that Luther was *born again* (twice born) in the way that Jesus talks about in the Bible, i.e., born into the spiritual (higher esoteric). However, the born again concept also works in our archetypal framework because we know that Luther was born again into the Orphan archetype. His earlier Orphan birth had been exoteric only. Now, he was born into the Orphan esoterically. Therefore, we place the event under the separation phase of the Orphan archetype as follows:-

Child	Orphan	Adult	Elder
	Separation	Transition	Incorporation

Luther rides into the storm. Lightning strike almost kills him	He promises to become a monk if saved	He joins the monastery

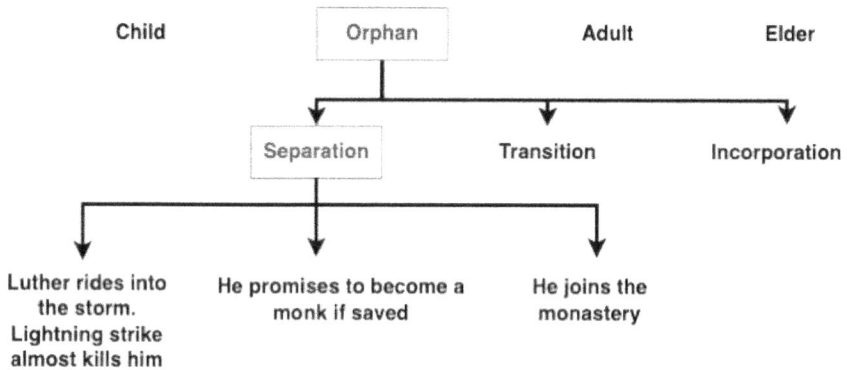

Thus, Luther's near-death experience in the forest was the esoteric equivalent of the Catholic rite of Confirmation in that he received the Holy Spirit directly. But the event also triggered the other main themes of the Orphan separation phase. By sacrificing his old exoteric identity, Luther initiated a break with his parents. His new identity as a monk would bring him into contact with the Elder (von Staupitz) whose guidance would prove crucial to his later Adult identity. Just as is required by the separation phase of the Orphan archetype, we see that the Child-Parent relationship was deprecated and the Orphan-Elder one established. But this was not done in the usual fashion by a socially recognised rite of passage but by a seemingly random act of nature. Let's return to the question we raised earlier: How could a random event become a cycle-ending-in-transcendence?

The short answer to that questions is that the trigger for a hero's journey may be random, but the hero is not. The hero begins the event in a certain state of being with a certain backstory and set of life circumstances. We know Luther was unhappy with his life. We know that he was dominated by his parents. We know that he lacked a meaningful Elder relationship. It is these factors which combine to create the hero's journey.

To appreciate the full meaning of this, let's now perform the same action we did earlier in our analysis of Confirmation and drill down one more level into the separation phase of Luther's hero's journey. This gives us the following diagram:-

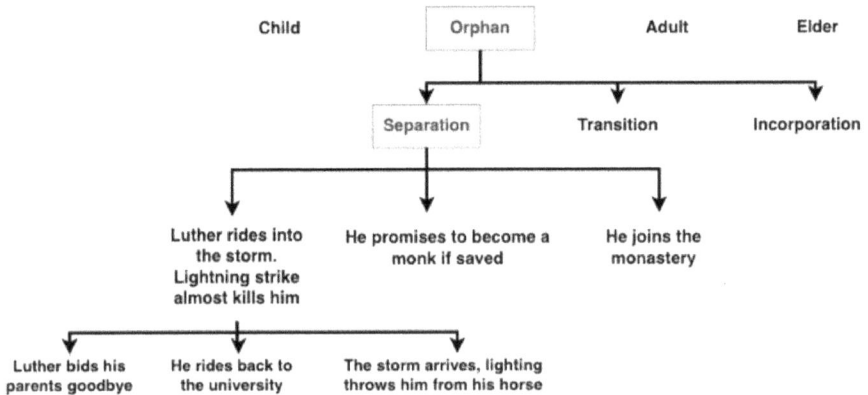

Once again, we see that this lower level of analysis provides only seemingly trivial information, but that's because we have yet again focused only on the exoteric actions that Luther carried out. If we think about the symbolic meaning of those actions, we get a very different picture. Luther is travelling from his parents house to the university. Why is he making that journey? Because his parents wanted him to become a lawyer. Therefore, he enrolled in university. The journey itself already implies the esoteric state that Luther was in. It is a microcosm of all the larger problems in Luther's life: the domination by his parents, his unhappiness at university, and his lack of wise Elder counsel. What are the odds that the lightning bolt would strike, literally and metaphorically, right through the heart of this dynamic, right in the middle of the house of Luther's parents and the university where their dreams of him becoming a lawyer were to be fulfilled? It seems impossibly coincidental. Yet, in terms of Luther's esoteric state, it makes perfect sense. He didn't want to be at university studying law. He wanted something more.

For our analysis of Confirmation earlier, we noted that the very first *separation* step is the decision to leave the house and travel to the church. At the physical level of being, such a statement is a tautology: *to get where you need to go, you have to start the journey.* But we know that the more important point is that the decision to go to church is esoteric in nature. Before we make the physical journey, we use our intent and our will to hold open a space in our lives. This space is sacred because we sacrifice our time to the rite of passage and to the higher esoteric belief system that it represents. It follows from this insight that the first step of the *separation* segment of a rite of passage occurs at the esoteric level of being. Could the same be true of a hero's journey?

At first glance, the answer would seem to be no, because unlike a rite of passage, a hero's journey is not organised in advance. That's especially true of events like Luther's near-death experience. Nobody could organise a lightning bolt to strike a particular place at a particular time (except God!). However, just because the specific details of the hero's journey cannot be organised or intended in advance, that does not mean there is no intent at all. In relation to Luther, we have already identified the key factors in his life. These form the esoteric background of the event.

A Catholic holds open a sacred intent to go to Mass or Confirmation. That is really the first link in the chain. It is what sets events in motion in the physical world. Luther, probably entirely unconsciously, must have had a similar intent to sacrifice his exoteric identity and become a monk. Even if the details of that intent were not clear in his mind, we know he was unhappy with his life circumstances. That dissatisfaction would have created a vague kind of intent, a desire for something more in life. It was this esoteric intent which Luther carried with him into the forest when the lightning bolt struck.

Even then, we must acknowledge how unbelievably coincidental it is that the lightning would strike just as Luther had said goodbye to his parents. That saying goodbye becomes the first physical link in the chain of events. The first move in the hero's journey is Luther leaving his parents so he can ride back to the university. At the time, that would have been completely unremarkable. Presumably he made that trip on a regular basis. Yet, a perfectly normal *separation* from his parents was about to turn into a higher-level *separation* at the archetypal level. The physical separation at the lowest level in the hierarchy transcends to the next level as a *separation* from normal, everyday life. The lightning strike created a sacred space by requiring of Luther a sacrifice. The sacrifice Luther offered caused a *separation* at the next level up. Luther decided to break from the exoteric identity that his parents had chosen for him. How incredible that he did this while riding to the university, an institution he was only enrolled in because his parents wanted him to!

Luther's sacrifice was, in fact, the sacrifice of the Child-Parent pairing in which he was stuck. But we know that the deprecation of the Child-Parent relationship is part of the *separation* phase of the Orphan archetype. We go up one more level and now arrive at the top level of the archetypes. Luther's hero's journey entailed a *separation* from his parents which began at the physical level and then transcended all the way to the archetypal. There are three levels of transcendence involved in this chain which we can map as follows:-

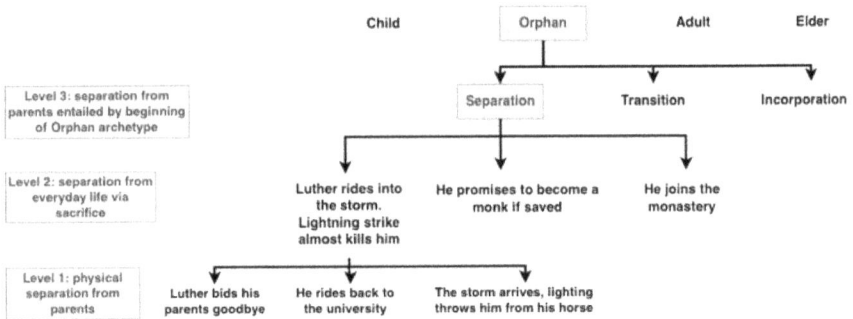

Luther separated physically from his parents by leaving their house to journey to the university. He separated from everyday life by finding himself in a life-and-death situation. He separated from his old exoteric identity, a relic of the Child-Parent relationship, and vowed to begin a new identity that he had chosen for himself. In doing so, he separated from the Child archetype, where he had been stuck psychologically, and began the Orphan archetype. None of this happened because of an exoteric, socio-cultural metamorphosis via a rite of passage. It happened because of an esoteric metamorphosis via a hero's journey.

Luther's story demonstrates perfectly the difference between the rites of passage and the hero's journeys while also showing that both can fulfil the same function of triggering the separation phase of the Orphan archetype. This raises the interesting question: are there two different ways to begin an archetypal separation phase? Is a rite of passage just as good as a hero's journey, and vice versa? Actually, the real difference here is our favourite distinction between the exoteric and esoteric. But what Luther's story shows us is that there is a certain type of character that prefers one or the other. This is the distinction we talked about earlier that William James made between the *once born* and the *twice born*.

For the once born, their socio-cultural identity is of prime importance, and, therefore, the rites of passage are enough for them because the rites confer social status. The once born happily accept the status given to them without questioning the higher esoteric belief structure implied by the rites of passage. They are the faithful and trustworthy members who form the foundation of any social institution. The twice born, on the other hand, need something more. That something is the higher esoteric. Like Luther, the twice born require esoteric initiation via a hero's journey.

Another way to think about it is in terms of what each character type considers a true sacrifice. Both rites and hero's journeys are cycles-ending-in-transcendence. We know that in order to be effective both require a sacrifice. For the once born, the sacrifice *is* their officially recognised position in a social group. The loss of the old social identity and the bestowal of a new one through the rites of passage produce a sacred response from such people because they value their social identity first and foremost. By contrast, an exoteric sacrifice is not enough for the twice born. They require something at the higher esoteric level of being. In the case of Luther, his experience in the forest was a sacrifice of his own life. We must believe that he really thought he was going to die. But his instinct in that moment was to appeal directly to his conception of the higher esoteric. It was St. Anne who saved his life and made him whole again. Therefore, it was St. Anne who conferred on him his new exoteric identity of monk. Luther was sacrificing his old exoteric identity, not as an end in itself, as it is for the once born, but in service to the higher esoteric. Luther really had received the Holy Spirit.

There is an interesting question here of whether the once born/twice born dichotomy is innate or learned. Do we come into this world with a *once born* kind of character, or do we become *twice born* through the circumstances of fate? Luther's experience in the forest seems to provide evidence that fate is the decisive factor, since a lightning strike is as good as a random event. But the biographical details we analysed earlier say otherwise. Luther was unhappy, stuck in the Child-Parent relationship, and living a life devoid of esoteric meaning. The lightning strike was random, but it was the trigger which unlocked the esoteric energy which had been building in the young man. It allowed Luther to manifest his true character as a twice born servant of the higher esoteric level of being.

Thus, our esoteric-exoteric dichotomy works to align the rites of passage and hero's journey with two distinct character types, each of which gravitates towards a particular kind of cycle-ending-in-transcendence. In both cases, however, the outcome is to initiate the separation phase of an archetype. Rites of passage such as Confirmation work in the socio-cultural domain to initiate those whose identity is dominant there. Hero's journeys like Luther's work in the higher esoteric for those whose identity resides there.

But far from being a minor psychological distinction that manifests as a preference for this or that mode of initiation, the once born/twice born dichotomy can be seen as a major factor in history, especially as it relates to the religious realm. The twice born regularly come into conflict with society precisely because their transcendence is esoteric in nature. Hero's journeys have no societal component and do not automatically confer social authority on the hero of the story. That is why the twice born find themselves so often in trouble with the official authorities of their time, for whom they are imposters. For their part, the twice born see that the rites of passage can only ever promise an initiation into the higher esoteric beliefs of a culture; they can never achieve it directly. As a result, the rites of passage always confer social status on people who do not deserve it. This is intolerable for those who understand what it means to have a connection with the divine.

The twice born live first and foremost in the higher esoteric. Given a choice between it and the needs of society, they choose the former. The truth is that, most of the time, society wins the battle against the twice born because institutions have more power than individuals. Every now and again, however, a twice born will tap into the *zeitgeist* and trigger a major change. Luther's esoteric transcendence in the forest is analogous to Jesus' confrontation with the devil in the desert, St. Paul's *road to Damascus* moment, and many other stories of religious revolutionaries throughout history. It also relates to fictional stories like King Lear and Oedipus. In fact, Luther's confrontation with the Pope is almost identical to Oedipus' confrontation with Creon in Sophocles' play. Even the tone of Luther's pamphlets is incredibly similar to the fire and brimstone that Oedipus hurls at Creon. We can hear the same tone multiple times in the Bible from various prophets. It is the railing of the twice born against the empty ceremonies and stale rites of a world that has become devoid of virtue.

In special cases, the arrival of the twice born is exactly what is needed either to reinvigorate the corrupt institutions of society or overthrow them in order to re-establish the higher esoteric. Although we won't be going into detail about this in this introductory work, what our analysis has revealed several times throughout this book is that there is another dimension above the individual, which relates to the collective of a society. Clearly, the lives of certain individuals resonate above and beyond their own circumstances and into the wider culture. If we posit that culture exists "above" the archetypes, then we could say that this is another level of transcendence. The story of Luther provides good reason to think that this is true because the aspects of his personal journey would become the aspects of Western culture more generally.

Luther's near death experience was the separation phase from his everyday life, which represented the separation phase of the Orphan archetype. Those separations led him onto a pathway of confrontation with the Pope, which in turn led to a revolution in the wider culture. Luther's *separation* from his parents turned into northern Europe's *separation* from the Catholic Church which, just like Luther's parents, only offered an exoteric existence, one that had become devoid of esoteric meaning. Thus, Luther's personal life journey became a microcosm for the larger social changes that took hold. We can see these correspondences more clearly when we connect the part of Luther's story we have just analysed with the part we told in chapter 4.

Given the extraordinary nature of the near-death experience and the fact that it unified both his esoteric and exoteric identities and set him on the life path of a religious anchorite, we might have expected that Luther's entry to the monastery would have been a great success. But we know from our earlier analysis that Luther was not spiritually fulfilled. It's not hard to see why. The monastery was always going to be a let down in comparison to the spiritual awakening the young man had experienced. Whatever rites were given to him by his Elders could never match what he believed was his direct connection to the divine. The reason why Luther pushed himself so much harder than his fellow initiates when carrying out his esoteric religious exercises was that he was trying to recreate the experience from the forest. But he never could. That was one problem that he faced.

The other problem was that his fellow monks had quite clearly not been inspired by divine intervention. Many of them treated monastic life more like an exoteric career path to be followed in the same way that Luther had once treated his potential legal career. Despite having gone through various rites of passage, Luther's colleagues were not in touch with the higher esoteric in the way that he was. They were once born, not twice born.

When he realised this, Luther drew the conclusion that the rites of passage themselves were worthless because they did not require any actual connection with the higher esoteric. Since rites of passage are always guarded and propagated by Elders, it is no surprise that Luther eventually turned his anger towards the Elders of the Catholic Church too. He ended up going to war against both the rites and the Elders, including the chief Elder himself, the Pope. All of this makes sense when we consider that Luther really did believe he had experienced a direct connection with the higher esoteric while the leaders of the church had not. This belief was not without some justification. In Luther's time, the Pope was barely a religious leader at all; he was more like a politician. To make matters worse, the church had invented rites of passage such as the indulgences, which were little more than naked exercises in money-grubbing. We might say that the Catholic Church as an institution had become once born. If the Elders of the church were themselves once born, then they selected Orphans of the same ilk. Luther was the twice born initiate who found himself in foreign territory. In exactly the institution where he rightly believed he should find the higher esoteric, he found its absence.

Because Luther could never experience inside the church what he had experienced outside of it, his initiation into the monastery was problematic from the beginning. In this respect, it was incredibly fortunate that the Elder he had been paired with, von Staupitz, was wise enough to see the problem. He advised Luther to ease up on the esoteric rites and return to academia. Luther rejoined university, now as a scholar of theology. Once again, we see how incredibly well Luther's life story fits our archetypal analysis. While he was at university at the behest of his parents, he was miserable. But when he returned, now under the guidance and counsel of von Staupitz, he thrived. Luther was not just a talented scholar but, more importantly, a great writer. It was his command of the German language that would eventually shoot him to fame. Combined with the arrival of the printing press, Luther's memorable writing style allowed him to run what was essentially a propaganda campaign against the church. Alongside his famous nailing of the theses to the church door, he wrote a number of incendiary pamphlets which took aim directly at the Pope.

The importance of the printing press cannot be overstated here. Numerous martyrs had taken on the church and lost in the centuries beforehand. Luther seemed destined for the same fate. His academic and theological objections would not have captured the public imagination, but his inflammatory pamphlets most certainly did. The reason why Luther's attacks resonated with the general public was that many of his fellow monks were not only not in connection with the higher esoteric; they were not upholding the basic standard of behaviour required of a holy person. Idleness and debauchery were not uncommon in the monasteries of the time, mirroring the corruption in Rome. Luther's personal circumstances gave him a borderline fanatical opinion on the issue, but the public knew that the church was mired in graft, and here was somebody who was trying to do something about it. Luther's deeply individual hero's journey turned him into a genuine hero among the general public for that reason.

The subsequent Protestant theology makes a great deal of sense when understood against this background, especially the personal lives of men like Luther. The Protestants did not just reject the corruption of the church, they rejected exoteric institutions and rites of passage altogether in favour of a direct connection with the divine. Luther had experienced that himself, and he believed that others should strive for the same. This tied in with the Protestant notion that the Bible was a way for the believer to directly access the word of God, without needing the church as an intermediary. Luther's translation into German, an act which had previously had many men declared heretics and put to death by the church, became a major turning point since it made the book accessible to lay readers and not just specialists trained in Latin or Greek. Combined with the new technology of the printing press, all of this really did break the church's stranglehold over access to the higher esoteric and made Protestant ideals a reality.

And this is where we return to the point made earlier in the book about the absence of Elders in modern Western culture. We can see why this development began with the Reformation's rejection of the Elder of the church, including the chief Elder, the Pope. Other seemingly unrelated factors of western culture also arose at this time. The high literacy rate in the modern West can be tied back to the desire on the part of the Protestants to have a direct connection with the word of God. Becoming literate in order to read the Bible was a skill pursued with religious fever. With high literacy levels, the success of the printing press was all but guaranteed and, in turn, created the modern news media. Much of modern education is predicated not just on literacy but the whole idea of learning through reading source material directly and forming one's own opinions on things. That, too, is a Protestant ideal. All of these factors were present in the life of Luther before they became properties of the culture more generally. Thus, Luther hero's journey transcended beyond his own circumstances and he became an archetype of modern Western culture.

But perhaps the biggest shift that Luther initiated is in the ascendancy of the hero's journey over the rites of passage. The absence of formal rites in the modern West is also a result of Luther's rebellion against the Catholic Church. For those us born into this culture, the major turning points in our lives are unlikely to be rites of passage formally marked out by our society but hero's journeys that are esoteric by nature. This is a genuine difference between modern society and the ancient world from which the Catholic rites of passage emerged. The ancients had no tolerance for the esoteric. For them, only what happened in public mattered. For us, it is very much the other way around. This is a defining feature of modern Western culture, and it began with the hero's journey of Luther.

The Final Transcendence

It is sobering to think that, for all our work in this chapter, we have focused only on the separation phase of the cycle-ending-in-transcendence for the Orphan archetype, exploring both its exoteric (Catholic Confirmation) and esoteric (Luther) manifestations. Even then, we only focused on the separation phases of the lower levels of that cycle, meaning there were eight other cycles we did not go into. And all of this analysis only referred to the religious-higher esoteric strand of identity that emerges with the Orphan. If we remember back to earlier in the book, the Orphan archetype also includes the development of biological, economic, political, military, and familial identities. We would be able to carry out the same analysis of the cycles-ending-in-transcendence that initiate each of these identities, including both exoteric and esoteric aspects. And, then again, all of this only relates to the separation phase of the Orphan archetype. We did not explore the transition and incorporation phases, and we did not apply the fractal cycle concept to the Child, Adult, or Elder, not to mention the question of the dual metamorphoses of the archetypal pairs and the important gender differences that we have touched on several times. The purpose of this book has been to give an outline of the model of archetypology and to demonstrate its validity. The fact that there are so many areas we have not investigated in any detail means there is plenty of work remaining for future archetypologists.

To use the catchphrase from this chapter, there is plenty more drilling down to be done. But we can finish this book with one more exercise in ascending the fractal tree. Remembering back to the point we made earlier about fractal cycles, we said that starting from any given cycle, we should be able to zoom in to lower-level cycles and zoom out to higher-level ones. We have provided ample evidence of the former, and we have seen the hierarchy of meaning that is created by the nested cycles of transcendence that connect the rites of passage and hero's journeys to the archetypes. But if the archetypes are themselves cycles-ending-in-transcendence, then we expect to be able to zoom out to find that they are part of a larger cycle. What should we call the cycle that sits above our four primary archetypes?

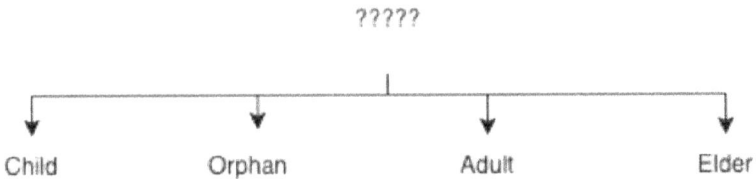

?????

| Child | Orphan | Adult | Elder |

But the answer is obvious. The four archetypes constitute the full human lifecycle. That is the cycle we see when we ascend the tree. It too is a cycle-ending-in-transcendence. We could call it a rite of passage. We could call it a hero's journey. But it seems most natural to call it an archetype: the Human archetype.

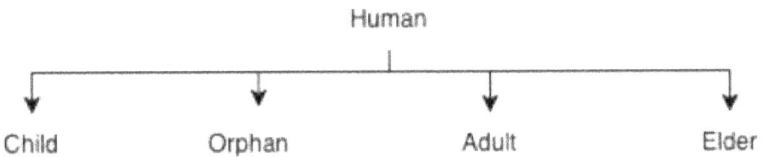

Human

| Child | Orphan | Adult | Elder |

It is the human archetype which governs the meanings of the archetypes below as well as all the rites of passage and hero's journeys down through the tree. Once we have completed the Child, Orphan, Adult, and Elder archetypal phases, we transcend to the Human, meaning we have fulfilled and sanctified all of the qualitative phases of the full human lifecycle. The completion of the journey is the summation of what it is to be Human.

Since this step concludes our model, it is also the summation of what archetypology is all about. For all of our work in this book, it turns out that our analysis really boils down to a single pattern, a single archetype. The ur-archetype of archetypology, the pattern which unites all the major concepts outlined in this book, is the fractal cycle-ending-in-transcendence. The evidence for the existence of this ur-archetype comes from a wide variety of disciplines, including biology, anthropology, comparative mythology, modern psychology, history, and others. When we place the ur-archetype at the centre of our analysis, the relationships between these disciplines become evident. Of course, we already have a name for them. We call them the humanities. Archetypology is the study of the human, and that is why the Human archetype sits at the top of our tree.

In archetypology, the unfolding of human development is our central concern. This unfolding occurs over the qualitatively unique phases of the archetypes, which consist of socially recognised ceremonies called rites of passage and spontaneous, personal episodes called hero's journeys. Because the hero's journey deals with the esoteric part of existence, it accounts for the individuality of every person. Sometimes, that individuality goes on to be codified in rites of passage. The great revolutions in human affairs are always stories before they are rituals. They are esoteric before they become exoteric. That is why we have named the highest level of being the *higher esoteric*. It is also why the rites of passage are geared towards the earlier phases of life, since it is here that individuals require structure and guidance. Later, our lives become far more like hero's journeys, meaning that they are centred more around esoteric, individual expression. Another way to put it is that we become more and more the author of our own story and less and less a character in somebody else's.

Of course, what almost every theology reminds us is that we are never fully our own author but always part of an even larger story. That is what Luther would have said and it's also what the Catholic Church would say. But even in a purely secular understanding, this is true because we are always born into a society and culture which was created by and propagated through our ancestors, whose own hero's journeys shape the structure of our lives, not just through the stories told about them but through their actions and deeds that leave a trace in our time. We owe our biological and cultural existence to these ancestors and perhaps far more of our esoteric existence than we are willing to admit.

This opens up the possibility that there is something more beyond the Human archetype. Although we have studiously avoided theological questions for most of this book, there remains an obvious possibility to be addressed. The Human archetype is also a cycle-ending-in-transcendence. We can drill down from it to find the four primary archetypes. But we know that we should also be able to zoom out from it to find a level "above" the Human? Does the cycle of transcendence that constitutes a human life end in one final transcendence? Is God waiting there for us to arrive, implying that he is outside of the cycle? Or is God the cycle itself? If the latter is true, then it follows that God really is present all the way down through the fractals, into our own lives, and into every action and experience as far as these represent the potential for transcendence. The rites of passage and the hero's journeys would then truly be sacred manifestations of the divine.

We will not attempt to deal with these issues here, but it seems a fitting way to end our introduction to archetypology to note that the model we have outlined in this book is not only compatible with these positions but lends itself to such conclusions. This will be something to explore in future works. For now, we simply note the possibility that the highest transcendence really is something like what the mystics, prophets, and theologians say it is.

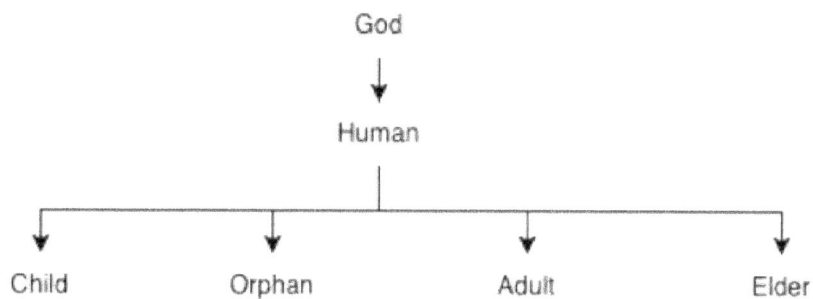

Epilogue

Now that we have defined the framework of archetypology, it is worth pondering to what uses it might be put. In the final chapter, we pointed out the areas of the model that we did not deal with in any great detail in this book. There is plenty of work there to investigate in more abstract terms how the hierarchies of meaning created by fractal cycles-ending-in-transcendence play out for the various archetypes. However, just as this book benefitted from using several case studies to make its points, we expect that any future work in archetypology would be well served by using the framework to shed light on real-world matters. Since archetypology aims for an integrated and holistic approach to understanding human development, we would expect it to be most applicable whenever a study of the whole life of a person is required. There are two primary disciplines where this holds.

The first is biography. Here we need to recall the point made earlier in the book about our modern conception of the difference between history as fact and literature as fiction. Biography used to be considered a branch of literature since literature was really just about narratives in general, and the distinction between real-life or fictional characters was less important. Nowadays, we tend to think that a biography should be based in fact, since we place it in the domain of history, and history is supposed to be scientific and verifiable. The trouble with that comes back to our distinction between the esoteric and exoteric. If we are judging a historical figure based on fact only, then we can only be judging them on exoteric criteria. This is why most historical scholarship is about specific events like great military battles, great political victories, or other tangible achievements.

There is an exoteric bias in such an approach due to the requirement to focus on facts. The only way to get around this bias would be to have access to the inner states of the individual concerned. Sometimes that is possible to do in a relatively rigorous fashion, most usually through access to letters and diaries or other lasting records of the inner states of the individual under study. Alternatively, the interpretation of those who are close to the individual can provide useful insights since those people are likely to have some appreciation of the esoteric dimensions of character. And, of course, there is also autobiography, which gives the individual's own explanation of events.

What we are concerned with in archetypology, however, are not only the events, and not only the subjective interpretations of them, but mostly how those events fit into the larger cycle of the life of the individual. In short, we are looking for the various cycles-ending-in-transcendence that structure a life. Much of biography and autobiography is not concerned with the relationship between events but only with the specifics, as if the events existed in isolation from each other. As an account of the achievements of the individual, this is fine. But as an analysis of the development of character, this does not work for us. Thus, we suggest that archetypology can improve on the usual form of biography by providing an explicit framework for the development of character over the course of a whole life. This can work even if we take a purely exoteric, or external, view of events.

The second discipline where we expect archetypology to excel is one that involves exploration of the esoteric side of human development, and that is the one we have focused on at length in this book—fictional stories. The freedom from overt concern over verifiable facts allows novelists and filmmakers the space to explore the subjective, inner dimensions of the human experience. Certain kinds of poetic and philosophical writing also fit into this category. The difference is that the latter are not expected to conform to the hero's journey structure, whereas the former are. Therefore, what we find in stories are explorations of character development from the esoteric point of view.

This gives us two areas of study that we could expect archetypology to shed new light on: biography and literature/film. In fact, we have already seen numerous examples of this in our analysis. What's more, we also saw some obvious parallels between the fictional and the real, for example, in the striking similarities between the stories of King Lear and Oedipus and the real-world stories of various religious figures such as Martin Luther, Jesus, and St. Francis of Assisi.

What archetypology can bring to the table here is the specific set of analytical tools laid out in this book, as well as the integrated approach to character development based around the archetypes. These can provide a new perspective on old questions. For example, Freud unsurprisingly analysed the story of Shakespeare's Hamlet as being an example of an unresolved Oedipus Complex. Our archetypal framework would disagree with this conclusion. We would see Hamlet as being the Orphan whose Adult identity has been usurped by his uncle, Claudius. Hamlet's problem is not a psychological hangover from childhood but a real-time problem of a failed Orphan transition, meaning that Hamlet is stuck in the Child phase of life. This analysis is backed up by the fact that Hamlet's would-be Elders, Claudius and Polonius, are actively working against him. Thus, his Orphan transition has been blocked by the lack of an Orphan-Elder relationship.

Archetypology not only allows us to identify such problems with precision, it also enables comparisons between like cases. In the fictional realm, we would say that Hamlet, Ophelia, Romeo, and Juliet all have the same problem: the absence of an Orphan-Elder relationship. It's the same issue that affected Martin Luther and Ida Bauer, to take two real-world examples we covered earlier in the book. What they all have in common is a problem during the Orphan phase of life that manifests as a dependency on the parents, often leading to a dramatic attempt to break free. The case of Luther provides a variation on the same dynamic.

Another dynamic which we didn't address in this book but which appears to be common is a dramatic break in the Orphan-Elder relationship, similar to the one that can occur when a Child-Parent relationship has extended beyond its appropriate duration. Two very similar famous examples of this can be seen in the stories of Freud and Jung and also between the philosopher

Nietzsche and the composer Wagner. In both of these cases, we see a situation where the Orphan needed to break free of the Elder in order to pursue their own ideas (and graduate to the Adult archetype). Much like the Parent must let go of the Child, the Elder must eventually allow the Orphan their freedom. If they don't, the Orphan may make the break themselves. Jung and Nietzsche had to break with their respective Elders to pursue their own journeys.

Archetypology takes freely from both fiction and biography because we understand the difference between the esoteric and the exoteric. We trust that the great works of fiction are great because they tap into truths that we know from intuition rather than from empirical verification. Nevertheless, such truths are also amenable to a kind of verification if we find them in the life stories of numerous, unrelated individuals, as the above examples show.

Although it could be true to say that archetypology has something to contribute to both biographical studies and literary studies, we could just as easily turn this around and say that biography and literature are the two main kinds of source material that archetypology makes use of because they are already tailored to a holistic view of the human. Archetypology uses biography and literature in order to improve and enhance our model of what it is to be human. We can also take from other disciplines such as Jungian psychology, biology, etc., where it is appropriate to supplement our work.

For these reasons, it makes sense that the next works within the archetypology paradigm will focus both on biography and literature with the aim of proving the validity of the framework. To the extent that our analytical tools can find new insights in such well-studied areas as a Shakespeare play or a famous biography, these will cumulatively add to the model's veracity. That will be the goal of future works in archetypology.

About the Author

For news on upcoming releases and regular blog posts, check out Simon's website at https://simonsheridan.me

Also by Simon Sheridan

The Universal State of America: An Archetypal Calculus of Western Civilisation

In this sequel to his 2021 book, The Devouring Mother: The Collective Unconscious in the Time of Corona, author Simon Sheridan follows the archetypal breadcrumbs in search of the historical basis for the psychological drivers that increasingly dominate our modern world. The Universal State of America is a brilliant work of synthesis, which argues that modern Western culture must be understood as a rebellion against the archetypal Father, leading to a unique form of empire based on feminine forms of dominance.

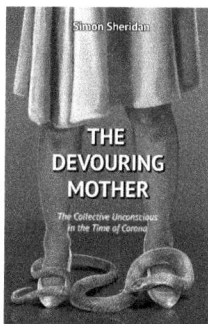

The Devouring Mother: The Collective Unconscious in the Time of Corona

Drawing on the work of the great Swiss psychologist, Carl Jung, The Devouring Mother argues that the archetype that has been dominant in the West for several decades is the Devouring Mother, a shadow form whose primary qualities include gaslighting, emotional manipulation and guilt tripping all in the name of protecting her children. The books connects the dots between seemingly unrelated social phenomena including politics, family, and broader social trends arguing that the time has come for the West to face its Jungian shadow: The Devouring Mother.

www.ingramcontent.com/pod-product-compliance
Lightning Source LLC
Chambersburg PA
CBHW072132020426
42334CB00018B/1772